Ninja Foodi 2-Basket Air Fryer Cookbook 2023

365 Days Quick & Easy Air Fryer Recipes for Busy People to Master 2-Basket Ninja Air Fryer

James Higgins

Copyright© 2022 By James Higgins

All rights reserved worldwide.

No part of this book may be reproduced or transmitted in any form or by any means, electronic or mechanical, including photo- copying, recording or by any information storage and retrieval system, without written permission from the publisher, except for the inclusion of brief quotations in a review.

Warning-Disclaimer

The purpose of this book is to educate and entertain. The author or publisher does not guarantee that anyone following the techniques, suggestions, tips, ideas, or strategies will become successful. The author and publisher shall have neither liability or responsibility to anyone with respect to any loss or damage caused, or alleged to be caused, directly or indirectly by the information contained in this book.

Table of Contents

Introduction 1

Chapter 1 Your Complete Guide to Ninja Foodi Two Basket Air Fryer 2

Unrivaled Dual Zone Technology 3
Features of Ninja Foodi Two Basket Air Fryer 3
Best Food to Cook with Air Fryer 4
Cleaning and Maintaining Tips 5

Chapter 2 Breakfasts 6

Bacon and Spinach Egg Muffins 7
Portobello Eggs Benedict and Mexican Breakfast Pepper Rings 7
Cheesy Cauliflower "Hash Browns" 7
Spinach and Mushroom Mini Quiche 7
Homemade Toaster Pastries 8
Egg in a Hole and Bourbon Vanilla French Toast 8
Turkey Breakfast Sausage Patties 8
Parmesan Sausage Egg Muffins & Pita and Pepperoni Pizza 8
Cheesy Bell Pepper Eggs 9
Savory Sweet Potato Hash 9
Baked Peach Oatmeal & Oat and Chia Porridge 9
Potatoes Lyonnaise 9
Cheddar-Ham-Corn Muffins 9
Homemade Cherry Breakfast Tarts 10
Sausage Egg Cup 10
Bacon Eggs on the Go and Cheesy Scrambled Eggs 10
Spinach and Bacon Roll-ups 10
Mini Shrimp Frittata 10
Breakfast Meatballs 11
Cinnamon Rolls 11
Mississippi Spice Muffins 11
French Toast Sticks 11
Mushroom-and-Tomato Stuffed Hash Browns 11
Italian Egg Cups 12
Bacon, Egg, and Cheese Roll Ups 12
Whole Wheat Banana-Walnut Bread 12
Whole Wheat Blueberry Muffins 12
Blueberry Cobbler 12
Pumpkin Donut Holes 13

Chapter 3 Vegetables and Sides 14

Cheddar Broccoli with Bacon and Tofu Bites 15
Lemon-Garlic Mushrooms 15
Blistered Shishito Peppers with Lime Juice 15
Chermoula-Roasted Beets 15
Spinach and Cheese Stuffed Tomatoes and Glazed Sweet Potato Bites 16
Hasselback Potatoes with Chive Pesto 16
Zesty Fried Asparagus and Five-Spice Roasted Sweet Potatoes 16
Garlic Roasted Broccoli 16
Garlic Zucchini and Red Peppers and Fried Asparagus 17
Hawaiian Brown Rice 17
Balsamic Brussels Sprouts 17
Crispy Garlic Sliced Eggplant and Cauliflower Rice Balls 17
Creamed Asparagus 18
Fig, Chickpea, and Arugula Salad 18
Butternut Squash Croquettes 18
Roasted Garlic and Lebanese Baba Ghanoush 18
Tamarind Sweet Potatoes 18
Broccoli Tots 19
Sweet-and-Sour Brussels Sprouts and Mushrooms with Goat Cheese 19
Garlic-Parmesan Jícama Fries 19
Parmesan-Thyme Butternut Squash and Roasted Pearl Onions 19
Roasted Grape Tomatoes and Asparagus 20
Baked Jalapeño and Cheese Cauliflower Mash 20
Garlic Fried Cabbage and Crispy Zucchini Sticks 20
Golden Garlicky Mushrooms and Simple Zucchini Crisps 20
Corn Croquettes 20
Crispy Green Beans and Lush Vegetable Salad 21
Garlic Herb Radishes and Ratatouille 21
Parmesan and Herb Sweet Potatoes 21

Fried Zucchini Salad 21
Radish Chips 21
Saltine Wax Beans 22
Indian Eggplant Bharta 22

Chapter 4 Fish and Seafood 23

Tuna and Fruit Kebabs and Parmesan Mackerel with Coriander 24
Crustless Shrimp Quiche and Shrimp with Swiss Chard 24
Cilantro Lime Baked Salmon and Almond Pesto Salmon 24
Sweet Tilapia Fillets 25
Shrimp Bake 25
Cod with Jalapeño 25
Tandoori Shrimp 25
Garlic Lemon Scallops 25
South Indian Fried Fish 25
Blackened Fish 26
Tuna Patty Sliders 26
Air Fried Spring Rolls 26
Lemony Shrimp and Zucchini 26
Cod with Creamy Mustard Sauce 26
Sea Bass with Roasted Root Vegetables 27
Catfish Bites 27
Shrimp and Cherry Tomato Kebabs 27
Balsamic Tilapia 27
Paprika Crab Burgers 27
Crispy Herbed Salmon 27
Honey-Glazed Salmon 28
BBQ Shrimp with Creole Butter Sauce and Fish Fillets with Lemon-Dill Sauce 28
Snapper with Fruit 28
Fish Taco Bowl 28
Parmesan Lobster Tails 28
Confetti Salmon Burgers 29
Spinach Scallops and Lemon-Tarragon Fish en Papillote 29
Garlicky Cod Fillets 29
Marinated Swordfish Skewers 29
Shrimp Caesar Salad 30
Popcorn Crawfish and Tandoori-Spiced Salmon 30
Fish Tacos with Jalapeño-Lime Sauce 30
Pecan-Crusted Tilapia 31
Country Shrimp 31

Chapter 5 Poultry 32

Butter and Bacon Chicken 33
Porchetta-Style Chicken Breasts 33
Chicken Schnitzel 33
Bacon-Wrapped Chicken Breasts Rolls 33
Gold Livers 34
Honey-Glazed Chicken Thighs and Peachy Chicken Chunks with Cherries 34
Apricot Chicken and Jerk Chicken Kebabs 34
Hoisin Turkey Burgers 34
Lemon Chicken 35
Spice-Rubbed Chicken Thighs and Herb-Buttermilk Chicken Breast 35
Spice-Rubbed Turkey Breast 35
Cracked-Pepper Chicken Wings and Buffalo Chicken Cheese Sticks 35
Yakitori 36
Easy Turkey Tenderloin 36
Jerk Chicken Thighs 36
Brazilian Tempero Baiano Chicken Drumsticks 36
Tandoori Chicken 36
Broccoli Cheese Chicken 37
Teriyaki Chicken Legs and Bell Pepper Stuffed Chicken Roll-Ups 37
Sweet and Spicy Turkey Meatballs 37
South Indian Pepper Chicken 37
Nashville Hot Chicken 38
Stuffed Chicken Florentine 38
Blackened Cajun Chicken Tenders 38
Cobb Salad 38
Chicken Wings with Piri Piri Sauce 39
Buttermilk-Fried Drumsticks and Garlic Soy Chicken Thighs 39
Wild Rice and Kale Stuffed Chicken Thighs 39
Buffalo Chicken Wings 39
Peruvian Chicken with Green Herb Sauce 40
Quick Chicken Fajitas and Greek Chicken Souvlaki 40
Yellow Curry Chicken Thighs with Peanuts 40
Chicken Legs with Leeks 40

Chapter 6 Beef, Pork, and Lamb 41

Easy Lamb Chops with Asparagus and Pigs in a Blanket 42
Teriyaki Rump Steak and Italian Lamb Chops 42
Chinese-Style Baby Back Ribs 42
Chuck Kebab with Arugula 42

Reuben Beef Rolls with Thousand Island Sauce 43
Greek Lamb Pita Pockets 43
Chorizo and Beef Burger 43
Parmesan Herb Filet Mignon 43
Tenderloin with Crispy Shallots 43
Blackened Steak Nuggets and Beef Loin with Thyme and Parsley 44
Swedish Meatballs 44
Pork Milanese 44
Korean Beef Tacos 44
Beef and Goat Cheese Stuffed Peppers 45
Jalapeño Popper Pork Chops 45
Cinnamon-Beef Kofta 45
Pork and Beef Egg Rolls 45
Herbed Lamb Steaks 45
London Broil with Herb Butter 46
Marinated Steak Tips with Mushrooms 46
Spice-Rubbed Pork Loin 46
Parmesan-Crusted Steak 46

Chapter 7 Snacks and Appetizers 47

Crunchy Tex-Mex Tortilla Chips 48
String Bean Fries and Spiced Roasted Cashews 48
Hush Puppies 48
Crispy Phyllo Artichoke Triangles 48
Roasted Mushrooms with Garlic and Lebanese Muhammara ... 49
Greek Street Tacos 49
Crunchy Chickpeas and Beef and Mango Skewers 49
Cheesy Zucchini Tots 49
Fried Artichoke Hearts 50
Greens Chips with Curried Yogurt Sauce 50
Mozzarella Arancini 50
Spinach and Crab Meat Cups 50
Pickle Chips 50
Skinny Fries 50
Shrimp Pirogues 51
Asian Five-Spice Wings 51
Corn Dog Muffins 51
Pita Flatbread and Sweet Potato Chips 51
Bacon-Wrapped Shrimp and Jalapeño 51

Chapter 8 Desserts 52

Vanilla Cookies with Hazelnuts 53
Butter Flax Cookies and Pumpkin Spice Pecans 53
Coconut-Custard Pie 53
Coconut Macaroons 53
Pecan and Cherry Stuffed Apples 53
Baked Brazilian Pineapple 54
Apple Wedges with Apricots 54
Gluten-Free Spice Cookies 54
Peach Fried Pies 54
Crustless Peanut Butter Cheesecake and Homemade Mint Pie 54
Butter and Chocolate Chip Cookies 55
Vanilla Scones 55
Almond Butter Cookie Balls and Coconut Flour Cake 55
Simple Pineapple Sticks and Honeyed Roasted Apples with Walnuts 55
Cream-Filled Sandwich Cookies 55
Fried Cheesecake Bites 56
Applesauce and Chocolate Brownies 56
Caramelized Fruit Skewers 56
Baked Peaches with Yogurt and Blueberries 56

Chapter 9 Staples, Sauces, Dips, and Dressings 57

Homemade Remoulade Sauce 58
Cauliflower Alfredo Sauce 58
Blue Cheese Dressing 58
Hemp Dressing 58
Orange Dijon Dressing 58
Pecan Tartar Sauce 59
Avocado Dressing 59
Sweet Ginger Teriyaki Sauce 59

Appendix 1 Measurement Conversion Chart 60

Appendix 2 Air Fryer Cooking Chart 61

INTRODUCTION

Do you struggle with weight as much as I do? Over the years, I have grown to both loves and hate food. I have found it extremely difficult to enjoy my favorite foods with the constant pressure of looking good and staying fit. Oh, how I would love to have a bucket of fried chicken!

Despite being a food aficionado, I have never been able to come up with a way to make food such as fried chicken much healthier. And to be honest, it is exhausting. For years, I have tried different recipes to ensure that I eat all my favorite foods and not gain weight, but all my experiments have gone down the drain.

I was disappointed with the taste of the food, but I ended up gaining weight. It is challenging for me to go on a diet and eat bland food as a foodie. This is where I completely gave up on the idea of healthy eating and succumbed to an unhealthy lifestyle that was full of fried food. It did make my heart more content, but I started suffering from severe health conditions.

Scared for my health and the future of my children, I had to look into different ways I could eat healthier food. This was when I came across the Ninja Foodi Two Basket Air Fryer. I was completely sold on the idea as this new gadget allowed me to eat all my favorite foods without worrying about packing on pounds.

Moreover, now I can try several recipes without feeling guilty and staying healthy for my family. Every meal is an exciting experience as I can use the gadget to create whatever I want, sans the hassle!

Chapter 1 Your Complete Guide to Ninja Foodi Two Basket Air Fryer

Chapter 1 Your Complete Guide to Ninja Foodi Two Basket Air Fryer

If you are looking for a gadget that does it all and gives you healthy food, then the Ninja Foodi Two Basket Air Fryer is something you'll regret missing out on. This appliance from Ninja Foodi is one of a kind, with two independent drawers and dual-zone technology. Using it is very convenient.

With the Ninja Foodi Two Basket Air Fryer, it is effortless for you to cut down on your fat intake and start your journey to health and fitness without depriving yourself of your favorite food. With many exciting features, this appliance is a worthy investment.

Unrivaled Dual Zone Technology

This particular appliance comes with dual-zone technology that utilizes two different cooking zones. This feature helps increase the versatility of the appliance. With the help of dual-zone technology, you can utilize two different cooking methods and cook two foods simultaneously.

Smart Finish

The best part about the dual-zone technology is that it ensures that both your two foods finish cooking at the same time. To cook both dishes at the same time, you can use their finish feature. Your food may have different cooking times or temperature settings to cook it, but with the help of the smart feature, you can easily adjust the settings to ensure that your food cooks at the same time.

Similar devices lack this particular feature that can make cooking so much more convenient. You no longer have to wait for the other dish to cook; you can cook both of them at the very same time.

However, if you do not want to use this feature or think that one dish is done before its time, you don't have to continue running the appliance. This might burn your food, and the Ninja Foodi 1 Drawer Air fryer gives you the option to 'Stop A Zone.' With this feature, you can set the time for one burner to zero so you can take the food out earlier and let the other one cook on its own time.

Match Cook

To get the full 8-qt capacity, you can also use the match cook button to copy the settings from one zone to another. This will help you match the cooking settings and cook both of your foods at the same time.

Such technology is an absolute benefit to have as it saves a lot of time and helps you cook more food in the same appliance easily.

Features of Ninja Foodi Two Basket Air Fryer

If you get your hands on the Ninja Foodi, you can benefit from many of its features. It is hard to find many of these features elsewhere; let's take a look at some of the most prominent features of the Ninja Foodi Two Basket Air Fryer:

2-Drawer cooking

Usual air fryers come with a single drawer cooking feature that can make it difficult for you to cook large batches of food or food with different cooking requirements. With its 2-drawer feature, you can cook two different types of food together and save up a lot of time. You typically do not get this feature in other air fryers and have to wait for one batch of cooking to complete so that you can start with the second one. This is why the 2-drawer cooking is a notable feature of the Ninja Foodi Two Basket air fryer.

6-in-1 Cooking Function

The multipurpose appliance allows you to cook food in six different ways, all in the same appliance. With the Ninja Foodi Two Basket Air Fryer, you can try the following cooking methods:

1. Air Fry
2. Air Broil
3. Roast
4. Bake
5. Reheat
6. Dehydrate

Less Fat

You may not know this, but even if you use different air frying techniques and appliances, you might still consume a lot of fat. This is where the Ninja Foodi Two Basket Air Fryer distinguishes itself from others. With this appliance, you will have 75% less fat than regular air fryers. This is a tested feature and has proven to be true.

Easy Cleaning

One of the very few cons of an air fryer is having difficulty in cleaning it. You may not know how to clean the air fryer properly, but with this appliance, you get easy-to-clean drawers, and the crisper plates are dishwasher safe, so you don't have to clean it on your own.

Best Food to Cook with Air Fryer

There are different kinds of food that you can cook with the air fryer; here are some of the best food options you can try:

Meat

If you are a meat lover and want to make a juicy steak, then you shouldn't shy away from using the air fryer. Other than a steak, you can also make several other meat dishes in the air fryer.

Fish and Sea Food

Many people like to include fish and other seafood in their diet but are unable to as cooking it may seem difficult. However, with the help of the Ninja Foodi Two Basket Air fryer, you can easily cook whatever seafood you want.

Vegetables

Steamed vegetables go wonderfully well with steaks. You can cook both your steak and steamed vegetables together using dual technology.

Fruit Dehydrate

Dehydrating food is, in fact, difficult, but with the help of the Ninja Foodi Two Basket air fryer, you can easily dehydrate any food you like.

Cleaning and Maintaining Tips

You may be hesitant to get the Ninja Foodi Two Basket Air Fryer as you may think it is difficult to clean it, but here are some tips you can use to clean and maintain it.

Use a damp cloth to wipe clean the main unit. Do not put the main unit in water or put it in the dishwasher.

To clean the crisper plates, you can wash them in the sink or put them in the dishwasher. You can towel or air dry them for the next time.

Clean the drawers by washing them by hand or by placing them in the dishwasher.

It is possible for the food to stick even after you have washed the drawers or the crisper plates. In this case, you can soak both of them in the sink with warm soapy water to soften the food.

Ensure that you unplug the unit when you start cleaning to avoid any mishaps.

You need to clean the unit after every use so that the food does not gather. This also prevents the bacteria from building up in the air fryer.

You can get further maintenance tips from the manual, or you can contact the team and ask them any questions you may have about the air fryer and ways to maintain its efficiency.

Chapter 2 Breakfasts

Chapter 2 Breakfasts

Bacon and Spinach Egg Muffins

Prep time: 7 minutes | Cook time: 12 to 14 minutes | Serves 6

6 large eggs
¼ cup heavy (whipping) cream
½ teaspoon sea salt
¼ teaspoon freshly ground black pepper
¼ teaspoon cayenne pepper (optional)
¾ cup frozen chopped spinach, thawed and drained
4 strips cooked bacon, crumbled
2 ounces (57 g) shredded Cheddar cheese

1. In a large bowl (with a spout if you have one), whisk together the eggs, heavy cream, salt, black pepper, and cayenne pepper (if using). 2. Divide the spinach and bacon among 6 silicone muffin cups. Place the muffin cups in the two air fryer baskets. 3. Divide the egg mixture among the muffin cups. Top with the cheese. 4. Set the air fryer to 300°F (149°C). Bake for 12 to 14 minutes, until the eggs are set and cooked through.

Portobello Eggs Benedict and Mexican Breakfast Pepper Rings

Prep time: 15 minutes | Cook time: 10 to 14 minutes | Serves 6

Portobello Eggs Benedict:
1 tablespoon olive oil
2 cloves garlic, minced
¼ teaspoon dried thyme
2 portobello mushrooms, stems removed and gills scraped out
2 Roma tomatoes, halved lengthwise
Salt and freshly ground black pepper, to taste
2 large eggs
2 tablespoons grated Pecorino Romano cheese
1 tablespoon chopped fresh parsley, for garnish
1 teaspoon truffle oil (optional)
Mexican Breakfast Pepper Rings:
Olive oil
1 large red, yellow, or orange bell pepper, cut into four ¾-inch rings
4 eggs
Salt and freshly ground black pepper, to taste
2 teaspoons salsa

Make the Portobello Eggs Benedict (zone 1 basket): 1. Preheat the zone 1 air fryer basket to 400°F (204°C). 2. In a small bowl, combine the olive oil, garlic, and thyme. Brush the mixture over the mushrooms and tomatoes until thoroughly coated. Season to taste with salt and freshly ground black pepper. 3. Arrange the vegetables, cut side up, in the zone 1 air fryer basket. Crack an egg into the center of each mushroom and sprinkle with cheese. Air fry for 10 to 14 minutes until the vegetables are tender and the whites are firm. When cool enough to handle, coarsely chop the tomatoes and place on top of the eggs. Scatter parsley on top and drizzle with truffle oil, if desired, just before serving.
Make the Mexican Breakfast Pepper Rings (zone 2 basket): 1. Preheat the zone 2 air fryer basket to 350°F (177°C). Lightly spray a baking pan with olive oil. 2. Place 2 bell pepper rings on the pan. Crack one egg into each bell pepper ring. Season with salt and black pepper. 3. Spoon ½ teaspoon of salsa on top of each egg. 4. Place the pan in the zone 2 air fryer basket. Air fry until the yolk is slightly runny, 5 to 6 minutes or until the yolk is fully cooked, 8 to 10 minutes. 5. Repeat with the remaining 2 pepper rings. Serve hot.

Cheesy Cauliflower "Hash Browns"

Prep time: 30 minutes | Cook time: 24 minutes | Makes 6 hash browns

2 ounces (57 g) 100% cheese crisps
1 (12-ounce / 340-g) steamer bag cauliflower, cooked according to package instructions
1 large egg
½ cup shredded sharp Cheddar cheese
½ teaspoon salt

1. Let cooked cauliflower cool 10 minutes. 2. Place cheese crisps into food processor and pulse on low 30 seconds until crisps are finely ground. 3. Using a kitchen towel, wring out excess moisture from cauliflower and place into food processor. 4. Add egg to food processor and sprinkle with Cheddar and salt. Pulse five times until mixture is mostly smooth. 5. Cut two pieces of parchment to fit the two air fryer baskets. Separate mixture into six even scoops and place three on each piece of ungreased parchment, keeping at least 2 inch of space between each scoop. Press each into a hash brown shape, about ¼ inch thick. 6. Place into the two air fryer baskets. Adjust the temperature to 375°F (191°C) and air fry for 12 minutes, turning hash browns halfway through cooking. Hash browns will be golden brown when done. 7. Allow 5 minutes to cool. Serve warm.

Spinach and Mushroom Mini Quiche

Prep time: 10 minutes | Cook time: 15 minutes | Serves 4

1 teaspoon olive oil, plus more for spraying
1 cup coarsely chopped mushrooms
1 cup fresh baby spinach, shredded
4 eggs, beaten
½ cup shredded Cheddar cheese
½ cup shredded Mozzarella cheese
¼ teaspoon salt
¼ teaspoon black pepper

1. Spray 4 silicone baking cups with olive oil and set aside. 2. In a medium sauté pan over medium heat, warm 1 teaspoon of olive oil. Add the mushrooms and sauté until soft, 3 to 4 minutes. 3. Add the spinach and cook until wilted, 1 to 2 minutes. Set aside. 4. In a medium bowl, whisk together the eggs, Cheddar cheese, Mozzarella cheese, salt, and pepper. 5. Gently fold the mushrooms and spinach into the egg mixture. 6. Pour ¼ of the mixture into each silicone baking cup. 7. Place the baking cups into the zone 1 air fryer basket and air fry at 350°F (177°C) for 5 minutes. Stir the mixture in each ramekin slightly and air fry until the egg has set, an additional 3 to 5 minutes.

Homemade Toaster Pastries

Prep time: 10 minutes | Cook time: 11 minutes | Makes 6 pastries

Oil, for spraying
1 (15-ounce / 425-g) package refrigerated piecrust
6 tablespoons jam or preserves of choice
2 cups confectioners' sugar
3 tablespoons milk
1 to 2 tablespoons sprinkles of choice

1. Preheat the air fryer to 350°F (177°C). Line the air fryer basket with parchment and spray lightly with oil. 2. Cut the piecrust into 12 rectangles, about 3 by 4 inches each. You will need to reroll the dough scraps to get 12 rectangles. 3. Spread 1 tablespoon of jam in the center of 6 rectangles, leaving ¼ inch around the edges. 4. Pour some water into a small bowl. Use your finger to moisten the edge of each rectangle. 5. Top each rectangle with another and use your fingers to press around the edges. Using the tines of a fork, seal the edges of the dough and poke a few holes in the top of each one. Place the pastries in the prepared basket. 6. Air fry for 11 minutes. Let cool completely. 7. In a medium bowl, whisk together the confectioners' sugar and milk. Spread the icing over the tops of the pastries and add sprinkles. Serve immediately

Egg in a Hole and Bourbon Vanilla French Toast

Prep time: 20 minutes | Cook time: 6 minutes | Serves 5

Egg in a Hole:
1 slice bread
1 teaspoon butter, softened
1 egg
Salt and pepper, to taste
1 tablespoon shredded Cheddar cheese
2 teaspoons diced ham
Bourbon Vanilla French Toast:
2 large eggs
2 tablespoons water
⅔ cup whole or 2% milk
1 tablespoon butter, melted
2 tablespoons bourbon
1 teaspoon vanilla extract
8 (1-inch-thick) French bread slices
Cooking spray

Make the Egg in a Hole (zone 1 basket): 1. Preheat the zone 1 air fryer basket to 330°F (166°C). Place a baking dish in the zone 1 air fryer basket. 2. On a flat work surface, cut a hole in the center of the bread slice with a 2½-inch-diameter biscuit cutter. 3. Spread the butter evenly on each side of the bread slice and transfer to the baking dish. 4. Crack the egg into the hole and season as desired with salt and pepper. Scatter the shredded cheese and diced ham on top. 5. Bake in the preheated air fryer basket for 5 minutes until the bread is lightly browned and the egg is cooked to your preference. 6. Remove from the basket and serve hot.
Make the Bourbon Vanilla French Toast (zone 2 basket): 1. Preheat the zone 2 air fryer basket to 320°F (160°C). Line the zone 2 air fryer basket with parchment paper and spray it with cooking spray. 2. Beat the eggs with the water in a shallow bowl until combined. Add the milk, melted butter, bourbon, and vanilla and stir to mix well. 3. Dredge 4 slices of bread in the batter, turning to coat both sides evenly. Transfer the bread slices onto the parchment paper. 4. Bake for 6 minutes until nicely browned. Flip the slices halfway through the cooking time. 5. Remove from the basket to a plate and repeat with the remaining 4 slices of bread. 6. Serve warm.

Turkey Breakfast Sausage Patties

Prep time: 5 minutes | Cook time: 10 minutes | Serves 4

1 tablespoon chopped fresh thyme
1 tablespoon chopped fresh sage
1¼ teaspoons kosher salt
1 teaspoon chopped fennel seeds
¾ teaspoon smoked paprika
½ teaspoon onion powder
½ teaspoon garlic powder
⅛ teaspoon crushed red pepper flakes
⅛ teaspoon freshly ground black pepper
1 pound (454 g) 93% lean ground turkey
½ cup finely minced sweet apple (peeled)

1. Thoroughly combine the thyme, sage, salt, fennel seeds, paprika, onion powder, garlic powder, red pepper flakes, and black pepper in a medium bowl. 2. Add the ground turkey and apple and stir until well incorporated. Divide the mixture into 8 equal portions and shape into patties with your hands, each about ¼ inch thick and 3 inches in diameter. 3. Preheat the air fryer to 400°F (204°C). 4. Place the patties in the two air fryer baskets in a single layer. 5. Air fry for 5 minutes. Flip the patties and air fry for 5 minutes, or until the patties are nicely browned and cooked through. 6. Remove from the baskets to a plate. 7. Serve warm.

Parmesan Sausage Egg Muffins & Pita and Pepperoni Pizza

Prep time: 15 minutes | Cook time: 20 minutes | Serves 5

Parmesan Sausage Egg Muffins:
6 ounces (170 g) Italian sausage, sliced
6 eggs
⅛ cup heavy cream
Salt and ground black pepper, to taste
3 ounces (85 g) Parmesan cheese, grated
Pita and Pepperoni Pizza:
1 teaspoon olive oil
1 tablespoon pizza sauce
1 pita bread
6 pepperoni slices
¼ cup grated Mozzarella cheese
¼ teaspoon garlic powder
¼ teaspoon dried oregano

Make the Parmesan Sausage Egg Muffins (zone 1 basket): 1. Preheat the air fryer to 350°F (177°C). Grease a muffin pan. 2. Put the sliced sausage in the muffin pan. 3. Beat the eggs with the cream in a bowl and season with salt and pepper. 4. Pour half of the mixture over the sausages in the pan. 5. Sprinkle with cheese and the remaining egg mixture. 6. Bake in the preheated zone 1 air fryer basket for 20 minutes or until set. 7. Serve immediately.
Make the Pita and Pepperoni Pizza (zone 2 basket): 1. Preheat the air fryer to 350°F (177°C). Grease the zone 2 air fryer basket with olive oil. 2. Spread the pizza sauce on top of the pita bread. Put the pepperoni slices over the sauce, followed by the Mozzarella cheese. 3. Season with garlic powder and oregano. 4. Put the pita pizza inside the zone 2 air fryer basket and place a trivet on top. 5. Bake in the preheated zone 2 air fryer basket for 6 minutes and serve.

Cheesy Bell Pepper Eggs

Prep time: 10 minutes | Cook time: 15 minutes | Serves 4

4 medium green bell peppers
3 ounces (85 g) cooked ham, chopped
¼ medium onion, peeled and chopped
8 large eggs
1 cup mild Cheddar cheese

1. Cut the tops off each bell pepper. Remove the seeds and the white membranes with a small knife. Place ham and onion into each pepper. 2. Crack 2 eggs into each pepper. Top with ¼ cup cheese per pepper. Place into the zone 1 air fryer basket. 3. Adjust the temperature to 390°F (199°C) and air fry for 15 minutes. 4. When fully cooked, peppers will be tender and eggs will be firm. Serve immediately.

Savory Sweet Potato Hash

Prep time: 15 minutes | Cook time: 18 minutes | Serves 6

2 medium sweet potatoes, peeled and cut into 1-inch cubes
½ green bell pepper, diced
½ red onion, diced
4 ounces (113 g) baby bella mushrooms, diced
2 tablespoons olive oil
1 garlic clove, minced
½ teaspoon salt
½ teaspoon black pepper
½ tablespoon chopped fresh rosemary

1. Preheat the air fryer to 380°F (193°C). 2. In a large bowl, toss all ingredients together until the vegetables are well coated and seasonings distributed. 3. Pour the vegetables into the two air fryer baskets, making sure they are in a single even layer. 4. Roast for 9 minutes, then toss or flip the vegetables. Roast for 9 minutes more. 5. Transfer to a serving bowl or individual plates and enjoy.

Baked Peach Oatmeal & Oat and Chia Porridge

Prep time: 15 minutes | Cook time: 30 minutes | Serves 10

Baked Peach Oatmeal:
Olive oil cooking spray
2 cups certified gluten-free rolled oats
2 cups unsweetened almond milk
¼ cup raw honey, plus more for drizzling (optional)
½ cup nonfat plain Greek yogurt
1 teaspoon vanilla extract
½ teaspoon ground cinnamon
¼ teaspoon salt
1½ cups diced peaches, divided, plus more for serving (optional)
Oat and Chia Porridge:
2 tablespoons peanut butter
4 tablespoons honey
1 tablespoon butter, melted
4 cups milk
2 cups oats
1 cup chia seeds

Make the Baked Peach Oatmeal (zone 1 basket): 1. Preheat the zone 1 air fryer basket to 380°F (193°C). Lightly coat the inside of a 6-inch cake pan with olive oil cooking spray. 2. In a large bowl, mix together the oats, almond milk, honey, yogurt, vanilla, cinnamon, and salt until well combined. 3. Fold in ¾ cup of the peaches and then pour the mixture into the prepared cake pan. 4. Sprinkle the remaining peaches across the top of the oatmeal mixture. Bake in the zone 1 air fryer basket for 30 minutes. 5. Allow to set and cool for 5 minutes before serving with additional fresh fruit and honey for drizzling, if desired.
Make the Oat and Chia Porridge (zone 2 basket): 1. Preheat the zone 2 air fryer basket to 390°F (199°C). 2. Put the peanut butter, honey, butter, and milk in a bowl and stir to mix. Add the oats and chia seeds and stir. 3. Transfer the mixture to a bowl and bake in the zone 2 air fryer basket for 5 minutes. Give another stir before serving.

Potatoes Lyonnaise

Prep time: 10 minutes | Cook time: 31 minutes | Serves 4

1 Vidalia onion, sliced
1 teaspoon butter, melted
1 teaspoon brown sugar
2 large russet potatoes (about 1 pound / 454 g in total), sliced
½-inch thick
1 tablespoon vegetable oil
Salt and freshly ground black pepper, to taste

1. Preheat the zone 1 air fryer basket to 370°F (188°C). 2. Toss the sliced onions, melted butter and brown sugar together in the zone 1 air fryer basket. Air fry for 8 minutes, shaking the basket occasionally to help the onions cook evenly. 3. While the onions are cooking, bring a saucepan of salted water to a boil on the stovetop. Par-cook the potatoes in boiling water for 3 minutes. Drain the potatoes and pat them dry with a clean kitchen towel. 4. Add the potatoes to the onions in the zone 1 air fryer basket and drizzle with vegetable oil. Toss to coat the potatoes with the oil and season with salt and freshly ground black pepper. 5. Increase the air fryer temperature to 400°F (204°C) and air fry for 20 minutes, tossing the vegetables a few times during the cooking time to help the potatoes brown evenly. 6. Season with salt and freshly ground black pepper and serve warm.

Cheddar-Ham-Corn Muffins

Prep time: 10 minutes | Cook time: 6 to 8 minutes | Makes 8 muffins

¾ cup yellow cornmeal
¼ cup flour
1½ teaspoons baking powder
¼ teaspoon salt
1 egg, beaten
2 tablespoons canola oil
½ cup milk
½ cup shredded sharp Cheddar cheese
½ cup diced ham
8 foil muffin cups, liners removed and sprayed with cooking spray

1. Preheat the air fryer to 390°F (199°C). 2. In a medium bowl, stir together the cornmeal, flour, baking powder, and salt. 3. Add egg, oil, and milk to dry ingredients and mix well. 4. Stir in shredded cheese and diced ham. 5. Divide batter among the muffin cups. 6. Place 8 filled muffin cups in the two air fryer baskets and bake for 5 minutes. 7. Reduce temperature to 330°F (166°C) and bake for 1 to 2 minutes or until toothpick inserted in center of muffin comes out clean.

Homemade Cherry Breakfast Tarts

Prep time: 15 minutes | Cook time: 20 minutes | Serves 6

Tarts:
2 refrigerated piecrusts
⅓ cup cherry preserves
1 teaspoon cornstarch
Cooking oil

Frosting:
½ cup vanilla yogurt
1 ounce (28 g) cream cheese
1 teaspoon stevia
Rainbow sprinkles

Make the Tarts: 1. Place the piecrusts on a flat surface. Using a knife or pizza cutter, cut each piecrust into 3 rectangles, for 6 total. (I discard the unused dough left from slicing the edges.) 2. In a small bowl, combine the preserves and cornstarch. Mix well. 3. Scoop 1 tablespoon of the preserves mixture onto the top half of each piece of piecrust. 4. Fold the bottom of each piece up to close the tart. Using the back of a fork, press along the edges of each tart to seal. 5. Spray the breakfast tarts with cooking oil and place them in the two air fryer baskets. Bake at 375ºF for 10 minutes. 6. Allow the breakfast tarts to cool fully before removing from the air fryer. 7. Make the Frosting: In a small bowl, combine the yogurt, cream cheese, and stevia. Mix well. 8. Spread the breakfast tarts with frosting and top with sprinkles, and serve.

Sausage Egg Cup

Prep time: 10 minutes | Cook time: 15 minutes | Serves 6

12 ounces (340 g) ground pork breakfast sausage
6 large eggs
½ teaspoon salt
¼ teaspoon ground black pepper
½ teaspoon crushed red pepper flakes

1. Place sausage in six 4-inch ramekins (about 2 ounces / 57 g per ramekin) greased with cooking oil. Press sausage down to cover bottom and about ½-inch up the sides of ramekins. Crack one egg into each ramekin and sprinkle evenly with salt, black pepper, and red pepper flakes. 2. Place ramekins into the two air fryer baskets. Adjust the temperature to 350ºF (177ºC) and set the timer for 15 minutes. Egg cups will be done when sausage is fully cooked to at least 145ºF (63ºC) and the egg is firm. Serve warm.

Bacon Eggs on the Go and Cheesy Scrambled Eggs

Prep time: 7 minutes | Cook time: 15 minutes | Serves 3

Bacon Eggs on the Go:
2 eggs
4 ounces (113 g) bacon, cooked
Salt and ground black pepper, to taste
Cheesy Scrambled Eggs:
1 teaspoon unsalted butter
2 large eggs
2 tablespoons milk
2 tablespoons shredded Cheddar cheese
Salt and freshly ground black pepper, to taste

Make the Bacon Eggs on the Go (zone 1 basket): 1. Preheat the zone 1 air fryer basket to 400ºF (204ºC). Put liners in a regular cupcake tin. 2. Crack an egg into each of the cups and add the bacon. Season with some pepper and salt. 3. Bake in the preheated zone 1 air fryer basket for 15 minutes, or until the eggs are set. Serve warm.
Make the Cheesy Scrambled Eggs (zone 2 basket): 1. Preheat the zone 2 air fryer basket to 300ºF (149ºC). Place the butter in a baking pan and cook for 1 to 2 minutes, until melted. 2. In a small bowl, whisk together the eggs, milk, and cheese. Season with salt and black pepper. Transfer the mixture to the pan. 3. Cook in the zone 2 basket for 3 minutes. Stir the eggs and push them toward the center of the pan. 4. Cook for another 2 minutes, then stir again. Cook for another 2 minutes, until the eggs are just cooked. Serve warm.

Spinach and Bacon Roll-ups

Prep time: 5 minutes | Cook time: 8 to 9 minutes | Serves 4

4 flour tortillas (6- or 7-inch size)
4 slices Swiss cheese
1 cup baby spinach leaves
4 slices turkey bacon
Special Equipment:
4 toothpicks, soak in water for at least 30 minutes

1. Preheat the zone 1 air fryer basket to 390ºF (199ºC). 2. On a clean work surface, top each tortilla with one slice of cheese and ¼ cup of spinach, then tightly roll them up. 3. Wrap each tortilla with a strip of turkey bacon and secure with a toothpick. 4. Arrange the roll-ups in the zone 1 air fryer basket, leaving space between each roll-up. 5. Air fry for 4 minutes. Flip the roll-ups with tongs and rearrange them for more even cooking. Air fry for another 4 to 5 minutes until the bacon is crisp. 6. Rest for 5 minutes and remove the toothpicks before serving.

Mini Shrimp Frittata

Prep time: 15 minutes | Cook time: 20 minutes | Serves 4

1 teaspoon olive oil, plus more for spraying
½ small red bell pepper, finely diced
1 teaspoon minced garlic
1 (4-ounce / 113-g) can of tiny shrimp, drained
Salt and freshly ground black pepper, to taste
4 eggs, beaten
4 teaspoons ricotta cheese

1. Spray four ramekins with olive oil. 2. In a medium skillet over medium-low heat, heat 1 teaspoon of olive oil. Add the bell pepper and garlic and sauté until the pepper is soft, about 5 minutes 3. Add the shrimp, season with salt and pepper, and cook until warm, 1 to 2 minutes. Remove from the heat. 4. Add the eggs and stir to combine. 5. Pour one quarter of the mixture into each ramekin. 6. Place 4 ramekins in the two air fryer baskets and bake at 350ºF (177ºC) for 6 minutes. 7. Remove the air fryer baskets from the air fryer and stir the mixture in each ramekin. Top each frittata with 1 teaspoon of ricotta cheese. Return the air fryer baskets to the air fryer and cook until eggs are set and the top is lightly browned, 4 to 5 minutes.

Breakfast Meatballs

Prep time: 10 minutes | Cook time: 15 minutes | Makes 18 meatballs

1 pound (454 g) ground pork breakfast sausage
½ teaspoon salt
¼ teaspoon ground black pepper
½ cup shredded sharp Cheddar cheese
1 ounce (28 g) cream cheese, softened
1 large egg, whisked

1. Combine all ingredients in a large bowl. Form mixture into eighteen 1-inch meatballs. 2. Place meatballs into the two ungreased air fryer baskets. Adjust the temperature to 400°F (204°C) and air fry for 15 minutes, shaking baskets three times during cooking. Meatballs will be browned on the outside and have an internal temperature of at least 145°F (63°C) when completely cooked. Serve warm.

Cinnamon Rolls

Prep time: 10 minutes | Cook time: 20 minutes | Makes 12 rolls

2½ cups shredded Mozzarella cheese
2 ounces (57 g) cream cheese, softened
1 cup blanched finely ground almond flour
½ teaspoon vanilla extract
½ cup confectioners' erythritol
1 tablespoon ground cinnamon

1. In a large microwave-safe bowl, combine Mozzarella cheese, cream cheese, and flour. Microwave the mixture on high 90 seconds until cheese is melted. 2. Add vanilla extract and erythritol, and mix 2 minutes until a dough forms. 3. Once the dough is cool enough to work with your hands, about 2 minutes, spread it out into a 12 × 4-inch rectangle on ungreased parchment paper. Evenly sprinkle dough with cinnamon. 4. Starting at the long side of the dough, roll lengthwise to form a log. Slice the log into twelve even pieces. 5. Divide rolls between two ungreased round nonstick baking dishes. Place the two dish into the two air fryer baskets. Adjust the temperature to 375°F (191°C) and bake for 10 minutes. 6. Cinnamon rolls will be done when golden around the edges and mostly firm. Allow rolls to cool in dishes 10 minutes before serving.

Mississippi Spice Muffins

Prep time: 15 minutes | Cook time: 13 minutes | Makes 12 muffins

4 cups all-purpose flour
1 tablespoon ground cinnamon
2 teaspoons baking soda
2 teaspoons allspice
1 teaspoon ground cloves
1 teaspoon salt
1 cup (2 sticks) butter, room temperature
2 cups sugar
2 large eggs, lightly beaten
2 cups unsweetened applesauce
¼ cup chopped pecans
1 to 2 tablespoons oil

1. In a large bowl, whisk the flour, cinnamon, baking soda, allspice, cloves, and salt until blended. 2. In another large bowl, combine the butter and sugar. Using an electric mixer, beat the mixture for 2 to 3 minutes until light and fluffy. Add the beaten eggs and stir until blended. 3. Add the flour mixture and applesauce, alternating between the two and blending after each addition. Stir in the pecans. 4. Preheat the air fryer to 325°F (163°C). Spritz 12 silicone muffin cups with oil. 5. Pour the batter into the prepared muffin cups, filling each halfway. Place the muffins in the two air fryer baskets. 6. Air fry for 6 minutes. Shake the baskets and air fry for 7 minutes more. The muffins are done when a toothpick inserted into the middle comes out clean.

French Toast Sticks

Prep time: 10 minutes | Cook time: 9 minutes | Serves 4

Oil, for spraying
6 large eggs
1⅓ cups milk
2 teaspoons vanilla extract
1 teaspoon ground cinnamon
8 slices bread, cut into thirds
Syrup of choice, for serving

1. Preheat the air fryer to 370°F (188°C). Line the two air fryer baskets with parchment and spray lightly with oil. 2. In a shallow bowl, whisk the eggs, milk, vanilla, and cinnamon. 3. Dunk one piece of bread in the egg mixture, making sure to coat both sides. Work quickly so the bread doesn't get soggy. Immediately transfer the bread to the prepared baskets. 4. Repeat with the remaining bread, making sure the pieces don't touch each other. 5. Air fry for 5 minutes, flip, and cook for another 3 to 4 minutes, until browned and crispy. 6. Serve immediately with your favorite syrup.

Mushroom-and-Tomato Stuffed Hash Browns

Prep time: 10 minutes | Cook time: 20 minutes | Serves 4

Olive oil cooking spray
1 tablespoon plus 2 teaspoons olive oil, divided
4 ounces (113 g) baby bella mushrooms, diced
1 scallion, white parts and green parts, diced
1 garlic clove, minced
2 cups shredded potatoes
½ teaspoon salt
¼ teaspoon black pepper
1 Roma tomato, diced
½ cup shredded mozzarella

1. Preheat the zone 1 air fryer basket to 380°F (193°C). Lightly coat the inside of a 6-inch cake pan with olive oil cooking spray. 2. In a small skillet, heat 2 teaspoons olive oil over medium heat. Add the mushrooms, scallion, and garlic, and cook for 4 to 5 minutes, or until they have softened and are beginning to show some color. Remove from heat. 3. Meanwhile, in a large bowl, combine the potatoes, salt, pepper, and the remaining tablespoon olive oil. Toss until all potatoes are well coated. 4. Pour half of the potatoes into the bottom of the cake pan. Top with the mushroom mixture, tomato, and mozzarella. Spread the remaining potatoes over the top. 5. Bake in the zone 1 air fryer basket for 12 to 15 minutes, or until the top is golden brown. 6. Remove from the air fryer and allow to cool for 5 minutes before slicing and serving.

Italian Egg Cups

Prep time: 5 minutes | Cook time: 10 minutes | Serves 4

Olive oil	4 teaspoons grated Parmesan cheese
1 cup marinara sauce	
4 eggs	Salt and freshly ground black pepper, to taste
4 tablespoons shredded Mozzarella cheese	Chopped fresh basil, for garnish

1. Lightly spray 4 individual ramekins with olive oil. 2. Pour ¼ cup of marinara sauce into each ramekin. 3. Crack one egg into each ramekin on top of the marinara sauce. 4. Sprinkle 1 tablespoon of Mozzarella and 1 tablespoon of Parmesan on top of each egg. Season with salt and pepper. 5. Cover each ramekin with aluminum foil. Place the ramekins in the two air fryer baskets. 6. Air fry at 350°F (177°C) for 5 minutes and remove the aluminum foil. Air fry until the top is lightly browned and the egg white is cooked, another 2 to 4 minutes. If you prefer the yolk to be firmer, cook for 3 to 5 more minutes. 7. Garnish with basil and serve.

Bacon, Egg, and Cheese Roll Ups

Prep time: 15 minutes | Cook time: 15 minutes | Serves 4

2 tablespoons unsalted butter	12 slices sugar-free bacon
¼ cup chopped onion	1 cup shredded sharp Cheddar cheese
½ medium green bell pepper, seeded and chopped	
6 large eggs	½ cup mild salsa, for dipping

1. In a medium skillet over medium heat, melt butter. Add onion and pepper to the skillet and sauté until fragrant and onions are translucent, about 3 minutes. 2. Whisk eggs in a small bowl and pour into skillet. Scramble eggs with onions and peppers until fluffy and fully cooked, about 5 minutes. Remove from heat and set aside. 3. On work surface, place three slices of bacon side by side, overlapping about ¼ inch. Place ¼ cup scrambled eggs in a heap on the side closest to you and sprinkle ¼ cup cheese on top of the eggs. 4. Tightly roll the bacon around the eggs and secure the seam with a toothpick if necessary. Place each roll into the zone 1 air fryer basket. 5. Adjust the temperature to 350ºF (177°C) and air fry for 15 minutes. Rotate the rolls halfway through the cooking time. 6. Bacon will be brown and crispy when completely cooked. Serve immediately with salsa for dipping.

Whole Wheat Banana-Walnut Bread

Prep time: 10 minutes | Cook time: 23 minutes | Serves 6

Olive oil cooking spray	2 tablespoons raw honey
2 ripe medium bananas	1 cup whole wheat flour
1 large egg	¼ teaspoon salt
¼ cup nonfat plain Greek yogurt	¼ teaspoon baking soda
¼ cup olive oil	½ teaspoon ground cinnamon
½ teaspoon vanilla extract	¼ cup chopped walnuts

1. Preheat the air fryer to 360°F (182°C). Lightly coat the inside of two 5 ½-by-3-inch loaf pans with olive oil cooking spray. 2. In a large bowl, mash the bananas with a fork. Add the egg, yogurt, olive oil, vanilla, and honey. Mix until well combined and mostly smooth. 3. Sift the whole wheat flour, salt, baking soda, and cinnamon into the wet mixture, then stir until just combined. Do not overmix. 4. Gently fold in the walnuts. 5. Pour into the prepared loaf pans and spread to distribute evenly. 6. Place the two loaf pans in the two air fryer baskets and bake for 20 to 23 minutes, or until golden brown on top and a toothpick inserted into the center comes out clean. 7. Allow to cool for 5 minutes before serving.

Whole Wheat Blueberry Muffins

Prep time: 10 minutes | Cook time: 15 minutes | Serves 6

Olive oil cooking spray	whole wheat flour, divided
½ cup unsweetened applesauce	½ teaspoon baking soda
¼ cup raw honey	½ teaspoon baking powder
½ cup nonfat plain Greek yogurt	½ teaspoon salt
1 teaspoon vanilla extract	½ cup blueberries, fresh or frozen
1 large egg	
1½ cups plus 1 tablespoon	

1. Preheat the air fryer to 360°F (182°C). Lightly coat the inside of six silicone muffin cups or a six-cup muffin tin with olive oil cooking spray. 2. In a large bowl, combine the applesauce, honey, yogurt, vanilla, and egg and mix until smooth. 3. Sift in 1½ cups of the flour, the baking soda, baking powder, and salt into the wet mixture, then stir until just combined. 4. In a small bowl, toss the blueberries with the remaining 1 tablespoon flour, then fold the mixture into the muffin batter. 5. Divide the mixture evenly among the prepared muffin cups and place into the two baskets of the air fryer. Bake for 12 to 15 minutes, or until golden brown on top and a toothpick inserted into the middle of one of the muffins comes out clean. 6. Allow to cool for 5 minutes before serving.

Blueberry Cobbler

Prep time: 5 minutes | Cook time: 15 minutes | Serves 4

⅓ cup whole-wheat pastry flour	½ teaspoon vanilla extract
¾ teaspoon baking powder	Cooking oil spray
Dash sea salt	½ cup fresh blueberries
½ cup 2% milk	¼ cup granola
2 tablespoons pure maple syrup	

1. In a medium bowl, whisk the flour, baking powder, and salt. Add the milk, maple syrup, and vanilla and gently whisk, just until thoroughly combined. 2. Preheat the unit by selecting BAKE, setting the temperature to 350ºF (177°C), and setting the time to 3 minutes. 3. Spray a 6-by-2-inch round baking pan with cooking oil and pour the batter into the pan. Top evenly with the blueberries and granola. 4. Once the unit is preheated, place the pan into the basket. 5. Select BAKE, set the temperature to 350ºF (177°C), and set the time to 15 minutes. 6. When the cooking is complete, the cobbler should be nicely browned and a knife inserted into the middle should come out clean. Enjoy plain or topped with a little vanilla yogurt.

Pumpkin Donut Holes

Prep time: 15 minutes | Cook time: 14 minutes | Makes 12 donut holes

1 cup whole-wheat pastry flour, plus more as needed
3 tablespoons packed brown sugar
½ teaspoon ground cinnamon
1 teaspoon low-sodium baking powder
⅓ cup canned no-salt-added pumpkin purée (not pumpkin pie filling)
3 tablespoons 2% milk, plus more as needed
2 tablespoons unsalted butter, melted
1 egg white
Powdered sugar (optional)

1. In a medium bowl, mix the pastry flour, brown sugar, cinnamon, and baking powder. 2. In a small bowl, beat the pumpkin, milk, butter, and egg white until combined. Add the pumpkin mixture to the dry ingredients and mix until combined. You may need to add more flour or milk to form a soft dough. 3. Divide the dough into 12 pieces. With floured hands, form each piece into a ball. 4. Cut two piece of parchment paper or aluminum foil to fit inside the air fryer baskets but about 1 inch smaller in diameter. Poke holes in the paper or foil and place them in the two baskets. 5. Put 12 donut holes into the two baskets, leaving some space around each. Air fry at 360ºF (182ºC) for 5 to 7 minutes, or until the donut holes reach an internal temperature of 200ºF (93ºC) and are firm and light golden brown. 6. Let cool for 5 minutes. Remove from the baskets and roll in powdered sugar, if desired.

Chapter 3 Vegetables and Sides

Chapter 3 Vegetables and Sides

Cheddar Broccoli with Bacon and Tofu Bites

Prep time: 25 minutes | Cook time: 30 minutes | Serves 6

Cheddar Broccoli with Bacon:
3 cups fresh broccoli florets
1 tablespoon coconut oil
½ cup shredded sharp Cheddar cheese
¼ cup full-fat sour cream
4 slices sugar-free bacon, cooked and crumbled
1 scallion, sliced on the bias
Tofu Bites:
1 packaged firm tofu, cubed and pressed to remove excess water
1 tablespoon soy sauce
1 tablespoon ketchup
1 tablespoon maple syrup
½ teaspoon vinegar
1 teaspoon liquid smoke
1 teaspoon hot sauce
2 tablespoons sesame seeds
1 teaspoon garlic powder
Salt and ground black pepper, to taste
Cooking spray

Make the Cheddar Broccoli with Bacon (zone 1 basket): 1. Place broccoli into the zone 1 air fryer basket and drizzle it with coconut oil. 2. Adjust the temperature to 350ºF (177ºC) and set the timer for 10 minutes. 3. Toss the basket two or three times during cooking to avoid burned spots. 4. When broccoli begins to crisp at ends, remove from fryer. Top with shredded cheese, sour cream, and crumbled bacon and garnish with scallion slices.
Make the Tofu Bites (zone 2 basket): 1. Preheat the zone 2 air fryer basket to 375ºF (191ºC). 2. Spritz a baking dish with cooking spray. 3. Combine all the ingredients to coat the tofu completely and allow the marinade to absorb for half an hour. 4. Transfer the tofu to the baking dish, then air fry in the zone 2 air fryer basket for 15 minutes. Flip the tofu over and air fry for another 15 minutes on the other side. 5. Serve immediately.

Lemon-Garlic Mushrooms

Prep time: 10 minutes | Cook time: 10 to 15 minutes | Serves 6

12 ounces (340 g) sliced mushrooms
1 tablespoon avocado oil
Sea salt and freshly ground black pepper, to taste
3 tablespoons unsalted butter
1 teaspoon minced garlic
1 teaspoon freshly squeezed lemon juice
½ teaspoon red pepper flakes
2 tablespoons chopped fresh parsley

1. Place the mushrooms in a medium bowl and toss with the oil. Season to taste with salt and pepper. 2. Place the mushrooms in a single layer in the two air fryer baskets. Set your air fryer to 375ºF (191ºC) and roast for 10 to 15 minutes, until the mushrooms are tender. 3. While the mushrooms cook, melt the butter in a small pot or skillet over medium-low heat. Stir in the garlic and cook for 30 seconds. Remove the pot from the heat and stir in the lemon juice and red pepper flakes. 4. Toss the mushrooms with the lemon-garlic butter and garnish with the parsley before serving.

Blistered Shishito Peppers with Lime Juice

Prep time: 5 minutes | Cook time: 9 minutes | Serves 3

½ pound (227 g) shishito peppers, rinsed
Cooking spray
Sauce:
1 tablespoon tamari or shoyu
2 teaspoons fresh lime juice
2 large garlic cloves, minced

1. Preheat the zone 1 air fryer basket to 392ºF (200ºC). Spritz the zone 1 air fryer basket with cooking spray. 2. Place the shishito peppers in the zone 1 basket and spritz them with cooking spray. Roast for 3 minutes. 3. Meanwhile, whisk together all the ingredients for the sauce in a large bowl. Set aside. 4. Shake the basket and spritz them with cooking spray again, then roast for an additional 3 minutes. 5. Shake the basket one more time and spray the peppers with cooking spray. Continue roasting for 3 minutes until the peppers are blistered and nicely browned. 6. Remove the peppers from the basket to the bowl of sauce. Toss to coat well and serve immediately.

Chermoula-Roasted Beets

Prep time: 15 minutes | Cook time: 25 minutes | Serves 4

Chermoula:
1 cup packed fresh cilantro leaves
½ cup packed fresh parsley leaves
6 cloves garlic, peeled
2 teaspoons smoked paprika
2 teaspoons ground cumin
1 teaspoon ground coriander
½ to 1 teaspoon cayenne pepper
Pinch crushed saffron (optional)
½ cup extra-virgin olive oil
Kosher salt, to taste
Beets:
3 medium beets, trimmed, peeled, and cut into 1-inch chunks
2 tablespoons chopped fresh cilantro
2 tablespoons chopped fresh parsley

1. For the chermoula: In a food processor, combine the cilantro, parsley, garlic, paprika, cumin, coriander, and cayenne. Pulse until coarsely chopped. Add the saffron, if using, and process until combined. With the food processor running, slowly add the olive oil in a steady stream; process until the sauce is uniform. Season to taste with salt. 2. For the beets: In a large bowl, drizzle the beets with ½ cup of the chermoula, or enough to coat. Arrange the beets in the zone 1 air fryer basket. Set the air fryer to 375ºF (191ºC) for 25 to minutes, or until the beets are tender. 3. Transfer the beets to a serving platter. Sprinkle with chopped cilantro and parsley and serve.

Spinach and Cheese Stuffed Tomatoes and Glazed Sweet Potato Bites

Prep time: 30 minutes | Cook time: 25 minutes | Serves 6

Spinach and Cheese Stuffed Tomatoes:
4 ripe beefsteak tomatoes
¾ teaspoon black pepper
½ teaspoon kosher salt
1 (10-ounce / 283-g) package frozen chopped spinach, thawed and squeezed dry
1 (5.2-ounce / 147-g) package garlic-and-herb Boursin cheese
3 tablespoons sour cream
½ cup finely grated Parmesan cheese
Glazed Sweet Potato Bites:
Oil, for spraying
3 medium sweet potatoes, peeled and cut into 1-inch pieces
2 tablespoons honey
1 tablespoon olive oil
2 teaspoons ground cinnamon

Make the Spinach and Cheese Stuffed Tomatoes (zone 1 basket): 1. Cut the tops off the tomatoes. Using a small spoon, carefully remove and discard the pulp. Season the insides with ½ teaspoon of the black pepper and ¼ teaspoon of the salt. Invert the tomatoes onto paper towels and allow to drain while you make the filling. 2. Meanwhile, in a medium bowl, combine the spinach, Boursin cheese, sour cream, ¼ cup of the Parmesan, and the remaining ¼ teaspoon salt and ¼ teaspoon pepper. Stir until ingredients are well combined. Divide the filling among the tomatoes. Top with the remaining ¼ cup Parmesan. 3. Place the tomatoes in the zone 1 air fryer basket. Set the air fryer to 350°F (177°C) for 15 minutes, or until the filling is hot.
Make the Glazed Sweet Potato Bites (zone 2 basket): 1. Line the zone 2 air fryer basket with parchment and spray lightly with oil. 2. In a large bowl, toss together the sweet potatoes, honey, olive oil, and cinnamon until evenly coated. 3. Place the potatoes in the prepared basket. 4. Air fry at 400°F (204°C) for 20 to 25 minutes, or until crispy and easily pierced with a fork.

Hasselback Potatoes with Chive Pesto

Prep time: 10 minutes | Cook time: 40 minutes | Serves 2

2 medium russet potatoes
5 tablespoons olive oil
Kosher salt and freshly ground black pepper, to taste
¼ cup roughly chopped fresh chives
2 tablespoons packed fresh flat-leaf parsley leaves
1 tablespoon chopped walnuts
1 tablespoon grated Parmesan cheese
1 teaspoon fresh lemon juice
1 small garlic clove, peeled
¼ cup sour cream

1. Place the potatoes on a cutting board and lay a chopstick or thin-handled wooden spoon to the side of each potato. Thinly slice the potatoes crosswise, letting the chopstick or spoon handle stop the blade of your knife, and stop ½ inch short of each end of the potato. Rub the potatoes with 1 tablespoon of the olive oil and season with salt and pepper. 2. Place the potatoes, cut-side up, in the zone 1 air fryer basket and air fry at 375°F (191°C) until golden brown and crisp on the outside and tender inside, about 40 minutes, drizzling the insides with 1 tablespoon more olive oil and seasoning with more salt and pepper halfway through. 3. Meanwhile, in a small blender or food processor, combine the remaining 3 tablespoons olive oil, the chives, parsley, walnuts, Parmesan, lemon juice, and garlic and purée until smooth. Season the chive pesto with salt and pepper. 4. Remove the potatoes from the air fryer and transfer to plates. Drizzle the potatoes with the pesto, letting it drip down into the grooves, then dollop each with sour cream and serve hot.

Zesty Fried Asparagus and Five-Spice Roasted Sweet Potatoes

Prep time: 13 minutes | Cook time: 12 minutes | Serves 8

Zesty Fried Asparagus:
Oil, for spraying
10 to 12 spears asparagus, trimmed
2 tablespoons olive oil
1 tablespoon granulated garlic
1 teaspoon chili powder
½ teaspoon ground cumin
¼ teaspoon salt
Five-Spice Roasted Sweet Potatoes:
½ teaspoon ground cinnamon
¼ teaspoon ground cumin
¼ teaspoon paprika
1 teaspoon chile powder
⅛ teaspoon turmeric
½ teaspoon salt (optional)
Freshly ground black pepper, to taste
2 large sweet potatoes, peeled and cut into ¾-inch cubes (about 3 cups)
1 tablespoon olive oil

Make the Zesty Fried Asparagus (zone 1 basket): 1. Line the zone 1 air fryer basket with parchment and spray lightly with oil. 2. If the asparagus are too long to fit easily in the air fryer, cut them in half. 3. Place the asparagus, olive oil, garlic, chili powder, cumin, and salt in a zip-top plastic bag, seal, and toss until evenly coated. 4. Place the asparagus in the prepared basket. 5. Roast at 390°F (199°C) for 5 minutes, flip, and cook for another 5 minutes, or until bright green and firm but tender.
Make the Five-Spice Roasted Sweet Potatoes (zone 2 basket): 1. In a large bowl, mix together cinnamon, cumin, paprika, chile powder, turmeric, salt, and pepper to taste. 2. Add potatoes and stir well. 3. Drizzle the seasoned potatoes with the olive oil and stir until evenly coated. 4. Place seasoned potatoes in a baking pan or an ovenproof dish that fits inside your air fryer basket. 5. Cook in the zone 2 air fryer basket for 6 minutes at 390°F (199°C), stop, and stir well. 6. Cook for an additional 6 minutes.

Garlic Roasted Broccoli

Prep time: 8 minutes | Cook time: 10 to 14 minutes | Serves 6

1 head broccoli, cut into bite-size florets
1 tablespoon avocado oil
2 teaspoons minced garlic
⅛ teaspoon red pepper flakes
Sea salt and freshly ground black pepper, to taste
1 tablespoon freshly squeezed lemon juice
½ teaspoon lemon zest

1. In a large bowl, toss together the broccoli, avocado oil, garlic, red pepper flakes, salt, and pepper. 2. Set the air fryer to 375°F (191°C). Arrange the broccoli in a single layer in the two air fryer baskets. Roast for 10 to 14 minutes, until the broccoli is lightly charred. 3. Place the florets in a medium bowl and toss with the lemon juice and lemon zest. Serve.

Garlic Zucchini and Red Peppers and Fried Asparagus

Prep time: 10 minutes | Cook time: 15 minutes | Serves 10

Garlic Zucchini and Red Peppers:
2 medium zucchini, cubed
1 red bell pepper, diced
2 garlic cloves, sliced
2 tablespoons olive oil
½ teaspoon salt
Fried Asparagus:
1 tablespoon olive oil
1 pound (454 g) asparagus spears, ends trimmed
¼ teaspoon salt
¼ teaspoon ground black pepper
1 tablespoon salted butter, melted

Make the Garlic Zucchini and Red Peppers (zone 1 basket): 1. Preheat the zone 1 air fryer basket to 380°F(193°C). 2. In a large bowl, mix together the zucchini, bell pepper, and garlic with the olive oil and salt. 3. Pour the mixture into the zone 1 air fryer basket, and roast for 7 minutes. Shake or stir, then roast for 7 to 8 minutes more.
Make the Fried Asparagus (zone 2 basket): 1. In a large bowl, drizzle olive oil over asparagus spears and sprinkle with salt and pepper. 2. Place spears into ungreased zone 2 air fryer basket. Adjust the temperature to 375°F (191°C) and set the timer for 12 minutes, shaking the basket halfway through cooking. Asparagus will be lightly browned and tender when done. 3. Transfer to a large dish and drizzle with butter. Serve warm.

Hawaiian Brown Rice

Prep time: 10 minutes | Cook time: 12 to 16 minutes | Serves 4 to 6

¼ pound (113 g) ground sausage
1 teaspoon butter
¼ cup minced onion
¼ cup minced bell pepper
2 cups cooked brown rice
1 (8-ounce / 227-g) can crushed pineapple, drained

1. Shape sausage into 3 or 4 thin patties. Air fry at 390°F (199°C) for 6 to 8 minutes or until well done. Remove from air fryer, drain, and crumble. Set aside. 2. Place butter, onion, and bell pepper in baking pan. Roast at 390°F (199°C) for 1 minute and stir. Cook 3 to 4 minutes longer or just until vegetables are tender. 3. Add sausage, rice, and pineapple to vegetables and stir together. 4. Roast for 2 to 3 minutes, until heated through.

Spinach and Sweet Pepper Poppers
Prep time: 10 minutes | Cook time: 8 minutes | Makes 16 poppers
4 ounces (113 g) cream cheese, softened
1 cup chopped fresh spinach leaves
½ teaspoon garlic powder
8 mini sweet bell peppers, tops removed, seeded, and halved lengthwise

1. In a medium bowl, mix cream cheese, spinach, and garlic powder. Place 1 tablespoon mixture into each sweet pepper half and press down to smooth. 2. Place poppers into the two ungreased air fryer baskets. Adjust the temperature to 400°F (204°C) and air fry for 8 minutes. Poppers will be done when cheese is browned on top and peppers are tender-crisp. Serve warm.

Balsamic Brussels Sprouts

Prep time: 5 minutes | Cook time: 12 minutes | Serves 4

2 cups trimmed and halved fresh Brussels sprouts
2 tablespoons olive oil
¼ teaspoon salt
¼ teaspoon ground black pepper
2 tablespoons balsamic vinegar
2 slices cooked sugar-free bacon, crumbled

1. In a large bowl, toss Brussels sprouts in olive oil, then sprinkle with salt and pepper. Place into ungreased zone 1 air fryer basket. Adjust the temperature to 375°F (191°C) and set the timer for 12 minutes, shaking the basket halfway through cooking. Brussels sprouts will be tender and browned when done. 2. Place sprouts in a large serving dish and drizzle with balsamic vinegar. Sprinkle bacon over top. Serve warm.

Crispy Garlic Sliced Eggplant and Cauliflower Rice Balls

Prep time: 15 minutes | Cook time: 25 minutes | Serves 8

Crispy Garlic Sliced Eggplant:
1 egg
1 tablespoon water
½ cup whole wheat bread crumbs
1 teaspoon garlic powder
½ teaspoon dried oregano
½ teaspoon salt
½ teaspoon paprika
1 medium eggplant, sliced into ¼-inch-thick rounds
1 tablespoon olive oil
Cauliflower Rice Balls:
1 (10-ounce / 283-g) steamer bag cauliflower rice, cooked according to package instructions
½ cup shredded Mozzarella cheese
1 large egg
2 ounces (57 g) plain pork rinds, finely crushed
¼ teaspoon salt
½ teaspoon Italian seasoning

Make the Crispy Garlic Sliced Eggplant (zone 1 basket): 1. Preheat the zone 1 air fryer basket to 360°F(182°C). 2. In a medium shallow bowl, beat together the egg and water until frothy. 3. In a separate medium shallow bowl, mix together bread crumbs, garlic powder, oregano, salt, and paprika. 4. Dip each eggplant slice into the egg mixture, then into the bread crumb mixture, coating the outside with crumbs. Place the slices in a single layer in the bottom of the zone 1 air fryer basket. 5. Drizzle the tops of the eggplant slices with the olive oil, then fry for 15 minutes. Turn each slice and cook for an additional 10 minutes.
Make the Cauliflower Rice Balls (zone 2 basket): 1. Place cauliflower into a large bowl and mix with Mozzarella. 2. Whisk egg in a separate medium bowl. Place pork rinds into another large bowl with salt and Italian seasoning. 3. Separate cauliflower mixture into four equal sections and form each into a ball. Carefully dip a ball into whisked egg, then roll in pork rinds. Repeat with remaining balls. 4. Place cauliflower balls into the ungreased zone 2 air fryer basket. Adjust the temperature to 400°F (204°C) and air fry for 8 minutes. Rice balls will be golden when done. 5. Use a spatula to carefully move cauliflower balls to a large dish for serving. Serve warm.

Creamed Asparagus

Prep time: 10 minutes | Cook time: 18 minutes | Serves 4

½ cup heavy whipping cream
½ cup grated Parmesan cheese
2 ounces (57 g) cream cheese, softened
1 pound (454 g) asparagus, ends trimmed, chopped into 1-inch pieces
¼ teaspoon salt
¼ teaspoon ground black pepper

1. In a medium bowl, whisk together heavy cream, Parmesan, and cream cheese until combined. 2. Place asparagus into an ungreased round nonstick baking dish. Pour cheese mixture over top and sprinkle with salt and pepper. 3. Place dish into zone 1 air fryer basket. Adjust the temperature to 350°F (177°C) and set the timer for 18 minutes. Asparagus will be tender when done. Serve warm.

Fig, Chickpea, and Arugula Salad

Prep time: 15 minutes | Cook time: 20 minutes | Serves 4

8 fresh figs, halved
1½ cups cooked chickpeas
1 teaspoon crushed roasted cumin seeds
4 tablespoons balsamic vinegar
2 tablespoons extra-virgin olive oil, plus more for greasing
Salt and ground black pepper, to taste
3 cups arugula rocket, washed and dried

1. Preheat the zone 1 air fryer basket to 375°F (191°C). 2. Cover the zone 1 air fryer basket with aluminum foil and grease lightly with oil. Put the figs in the zone 1 air fryer basket and air fry for 10 minutes. 3. In a bowl, combine the chickpeas and cumin seeds. 4. Remove the air fried figs from the air fryer and replace with the chickpeas. Air fry for 10 minutes. Leave to cool. 5. In the meantime, prepare the dressing. Mix the balsamic vinegar, olive oil, salt and pepper. 6. In a salad bowl, combine the arugula rocket with the cooled figs and chickpeas. 7. Toss with the sauce and serve.

Butternut Squash Croquettes

Prep time: 5 minutes | Cook time: 17 minutes | Serves 4

⅓ butternut squash, peeled and grated
⅓ cup all-purpose flour
2 eggs, whisked
4 cloves garlic, minced
1½ tablespoons olive oil
1 teaspoon fine sea salt
⅓ teaspoon freshly ground black pepper, or more to taste
⅓ teaspoon dried sage
A pinch of ground allspice

1. Preheat the zone 1 air fryer basket to 345°F (174°C). Line the zone 1 air fryer basket with parchment paper. 2. In a mixing bowl, stir together all the ingredients until well combined. 3. Make the squash croquettes: Use a small cookie scoop to drop tablespoonfuls of the squash mixture onto a lightly floured surface and shape into balls with your hands. Transfer them to the zone 1 air fryer basket. 4. Air fry for 17 minutes until the squash croquettes are golden brown. 5. Remove from the basket to a plate and serve warm.

Roasted Garlic and Lebanese Baba Ghanoush

Prep time: 20 minutes | Cook time: 20 minutes | Serves 7

Roasted Garlic:
1 medium head garlic
2 teaspoons avocado oil
Lebanese Baba Ghanoush:
1 medium eggplant
2 tablespoons vegetable oil
2 tablespoons tahini (sesame paste)
2 tablespoons fresh lemon juice
½ teaspoon kosher salt
1 tablespoon extra-virgin olive oil
½ teaspoon smoked paprika
2 tablespoons chopped fresh parsley

Make the Roasted Garlic: 1. Remove any hanging excess peel from the garlic but leave the cloves covered. Cut off ¼ of the head of garlic, exposing the tips of the cloves. 2. Drizzle with avocado oil. Place the garlic head into a small sheet of aluminum foil, completely enclosing it. Place it into the zone 1 air fryer basket. 3. Adjust the temperature to 400°F (204°C) and air fry for 20 minutes. If your garlic head is a bit smaller, check it after 15 minutes. 4. When done, garlic should be golden brown and very soft. 5. To serve, cloves should pop out and easily be spread or sliced. Store in an airtight container in the refrigerator up to 5 days. You may also freeze individual cloves on a baking sheet, then store together in a freezer-safe storage bag once frozen.
Make the Lebanese Baba Ghanoush: 1. Rub the eggplant all over with the vegetable oil. Place the eggplant in the zone 2 air fryer basket. Set the zone 2 air fryer basket to 400°F (204°C) for 20 minutes, or until the eggplant skin is blistered and charred. 2. Transfer the eggplant to a resealable plastic bag, seal, and set aside for 15 minutes (the eggplant will finish cooking in the residual heat trapped in the bag). 3. Transfer the eggplant to a large bowl. Peel off and discard the charred skin. Roughly mash the eggplant flesh. Add the tahini, lemon juice, and salt. Stir to combine. 4. Transfer the mixture to a serving bowl. Drizzle with the olive oil. Sprinkle with the paprika and parsley and serve.

Tamarind Sweet Potatoes

Prep time: 5 minutes | Cook time: 20 to 25 minutes | Serves 4

5 garnet sweet potatoes, peeled and diced
1½ tablespoons fresh lime juice
1 tablespoon butter, melted
2 teaspoons tamarind paste
1½ teaspoon ground allspice
⅓ teaspoon white pepper
½ teaspoon turmeric powder
A few drops liquid stevia

1. Preheat the zone 1 air fryer basket to 400°F (204°C). 2. In a large mixing bowl, combine all the ingredients and toss until the sweet potatoes are evenly coated. 3. Place the sweet potatoes in the zone 1 air fryer basket and air fry for 20 t0 25 minutes, or until the potatoes are crispy on the outside and soft on the inside. Shake the basket twice during cooking. 4. Let the potatoes cool for 5 minutes before serving.

Broccoli Tots

Prep time: 15 minutes | Cook time: 10 minutes | Makes 24 tots

2 cups broccoli florets (about ½ pound / 227 g broccoli crowns)
1 egg, beaten
⅛ teaspoon onion powder
¼ teaspoon salt
⅛ teaspoon pepper
2 tablespoons grated Parmesan cheese
¼ cup panko bread crumbs
Oil for misting

1. Steam broccoli for 2 minutes. Rinse in cold water, drain well, and chop finely. 2. In a large bowl, mix broccoli with all other ingredients except the oil. 3. Scoop out small portions of mixture and shape into 24 tots. Lay them on a cookie sheet or wax paper as you work. 4. Spray tots with oil and place in the two air fryer baskets in single layer. 5. Air fry at 390°F (199°C) for 5 minutes. Shake baskets and spray with oil again. Cook 5 minutes longer or until browned and crispy.

Sweet-and-Sour Brussels Sprouts and Mushrooms with Goat Cheese

Prep time: 20 minutes | Cook time: 20 minutes | Serves 6

Sweet-and-Sour Brussels Sprouts:
¼ cup Thai sweet chili sauce
2 tablespoons black vinegar or balsamic vinegar
½ teaspoon hot sauce, such as Tabasco
8 ounces (227 g) Brussels sprouts, trimmed (large sprouts halved)
2 small shallots, cut into ¼-inch-thick slices
Kosher salt and freshly ground black pepper, to taste
2 teaspoons lightly packed fresh cilantro leaves
Mushrooms with Goat Cheese:
3 tablespoons vegetable oil
1 pound (454 g) mixed mushrooms, trimmed and sliced
1 clove garlic, minced
¼ teaspoon dried thyme
½ teaspoon black pepper
4 ounces (113 g) goat cheese, diced
2 teaspoons chopped fresh thyme leaves (optional)

Make the Sweet-and-Sour Brussels Sprouts (zone 1 basket): 1. In a large bowl, whisk together the chili sauce, vinegar, and hot sauce. Add the Brussels sprouts and shallots, season with salt and pepper, and toss to combine. Scrape the Brussels sprouts and sauce into a cake pan. 2. Place the pan in the zone 1 air fryer basket and roast at 375°F (191°C), stirring every 5 minutes, until the Brussels sprouts are tender and the sauce is reduced to a sticky glaze, about 20 minutes. 3. Remove the pan from the air fryer and transfer the Brussels sprouts to plates. Sprinkle with the cilantro and serve warm.
Make the Mushrooms with Goat Cheese (zone 2 basket): 1. In a baking pan, combine the oil, mushrooms, garlic, dried thyme, and pepper. Stir in the goat cheese. Place the pan in the zone 2 air fryer basket. Set the air fryer to 400°F (204°C) for 10 minutes, stirring halfway through the cooking time. 2. Sprinkle with fresh thyme, if desired.

Garlic-Parmesan Jícama Fries

Prep time: 10 minutes | Cook time: 25 to 35 minutes | Serves 4

1 medium jícama, peeled
1 tablespoon avocado oil
¼ cup (4 tablespoons) unsalted butter
1 tablespoon minced garlic
¾ teaspoon chopped dried rosemary
¾ teaspoon sea salt
½ teaspoon freshly ground black pepper
⅓ cup grated Parmesan cheese
Chopped fresh parsley, for garnish
Maldon sea salt, for garnish

1. Using a spiralizer or julienne peeler, cut the jícama into shoestrings, then cut them into 3-inch-long sticks. 2. Bring a large pot of water to boil. Add the jícama and cook for about 10 minutes. Drain and dry on paper towels. Transfer to a medium bowl and toss with the oil. 3. Set the air fryer to 400°F (204°C). Arrange the jícama in a single layer in the two baskets. Air fry for 15 to 25 minutes, checking at intervals, until tender and golden brown. 4. While the fries cook, melt the butter over medium-high heat. Add the garlic, rosemary, salt, and pepper. Cook for about 1 minute. 5. Toss the fries with the garlic butter. Top with the Parmesan cheese, and sprinkle with parsley and Maldon sea salt.

Parmesan-Thyme Butternut Squash and Roasted Pearl Onions

Prep time: 10 minutes | Cook time: 20 minutes | Serves 7

Parmesan-Thyme Butternut Squash:
2½ cups butternut squash, cubed into 1-inch pieces (approximately 1 medium)
2 tablespoons olive oil
¼ teaspoon salt
¼ teaspoon garlic powder
¼ teaspoon black pepper
1 tablespoon fresh thyme
¼ cup grated Parmesan
Roasted Pearl Onions:
1 (14½-ounce / 411-g) package frozen pearl onions (do not thaw)
2 tablespoons extra-virgin olive oil
2 tablespoons balsamic vinegar
2 teaspoons finely chopped fresh rosemary
½ teaspoon kosher salt
¼ teaspoon black pepper

Make the Parmesan-Thyme Butternut Squash: 1. Preheat the zone 1 air fryer basket to 360°F (182°C). 2. In a large bowl, combine the cubed squash with the olive oil, salt, garlic powder, pepper, and thyme until the squash is well coated. 3. Pour this mixture into the zone 1 air fryer basket, and roast for 10 minutes. Stir and roast another 8 to 10 minutes more. 4. Remove the squash from the air fryer and toss with freshly grated Parmesan before serving.
Make the Roasted Pearl Onions: 1. In a medium bowl, combine the onions, olive oil, vinegar, rosemary, salt, and pepper until well coated. 2. Transfer the onions to the zone 2 air fryer basket. Set the temperature to 400°F (204°C) for 18 minutes, or until the onions are tender and lightly charred, stirring once or twice during the cooking time.

Roasted Grape Tomatoes and Asparagus

Prep time: 5 minutes | Cook time: 12 minutes | Serves 6

2 cups grape tomatoes
1 bunch asparagus, trimmed
2 tablespoons olive oil
3 garlic cloves, minced
½ teaspoon kosher salt

1. Preheat the air fryer to 380°F (193°C). 2. In a large bowl, combine all of the ingredients, tossing until the vegetables are well coated with oil. 3. Pour the vegetable mixture into the two air fryer baskets and spread into a single layer, then roast for 12 minutes.

Baked Jalapeño and Cheese Cauliflower Mash

Prep time: 10 minutes | Cook time: 15 minutes | Serves 6

1 (12-ounce / 340-g) steamer bag cauliflower florets, cooked according to package instructions
2 tablespoons salted butter, softened
2 ounces (57 g) cream cheese, softened
½ cup shredded sharp Cheddar cheese
¼ cup pickled jalapeños
½ teaspoon salt
¼ teaspoon ground black pepper

1. Place cooked cauliflower into a food processor with remaining ingredients. Pulse twenty times until cauliflower is smooth and all ingredients are combined. 2. Spoon mash into an ungreased round nonstick baking dish. Place dish into the zone 1 air fryer basket. Adjust the temperature to 380°F (193°C) and bake for 15 minutes. The top will be golden brown when done. Serve warm.

Garlic Fried Cabbage and Crispy Zucchini Sticks

Prep time: 10 minutes | Cook time: 14 minutes | Serves 6

Garlic Fried Cabbage:
Oil, for spraying
½ head cabbage, cut into bite-size pieces
2 tablespoons unsalted butter, melted
1 teaspoon granulated garlic
½ teaspoon coarse sea salt
¼ teaspoon freshly ground black pepper
Crispy Zucchini Sticks:
2 small zucchini, cut into 2-inch × ½-inch sticks
3 tablespoons chickpea flour
2 teaspoons arrowroot (or cornstarch)
½ teaspoon garlic granules
¼ teaspoon sea salt
⅛ teaspoon freshly ground black pepper
1 tablespoon water
Cooking spray

Make the Garlic Fried Cabbage (zone 1 basket): 1. Line the zone 1 air fryer basket with parchment and spray lightly with oil. 2. In a large bowl, mix together the cabbage, butter, garlic, salt, and black pepper until evenly coated. 3. Transfer the cabbage to the prepared basket and spray lightly with oil. 4. Air fry at 375°F (191°C) for 5 minutes, toss, and cook for another 3 to 4 minutes, or until lightly crispy.
Make the Crispy Zucchini Sticks (zone 2 basket): 1. Preheat the air fryer to 392°F (200°C). 2. Combine the zucchini sticks with the chickpea flour, arrowroot, garlic granules, salt, and pepper in a medium bowl and toss to coat. Add the water and stir to mix well. 3. Spritz the zone 2 air fryer basket with cooking spray and spread out the zucchini sticks in the basket. Mist the zucchini sticks with cooking spray. 4. Air fry for 14 minutes, shaking the basket halfway through, or until the zucchini sticks are crispy and nicely browned. 5. Serve warm.

Golden Garlicky Mushrooms and Simple Zucchini Crisps

Prep time: 15 minutes | Cook time: 14 minutes | Serves 8

Golden Garlicky Mushrooms:
6 small mushrooms
1 tablespoon bread crumbs
1 tablespoon olive oil
1 ounce (28 g) onion, peeled and diced
1 teaspoon parsley
1 teaspoon garlic purée
Salt and ground black pepper, to taste
Simple Zucchini Crisps:
2 zucchini, sliced into ¼- to ½-inch-thick rounds (about 2 cups)
¼ teaspoon garlic granules
⅛ teaspoon sea salt
Freshly ground black pepper, to taste (optional)
Cooking spray

Make the Golden Garlicky Mushrooms (zone 1 basket): 1. Preheat the zone 1 air fryer basket to 350°F (177°C). 2. Combine the bread crumbs, oil, onion, parsley, salt, pepper and garlic in a bowl. Cut out the mushrooms' stalks and stuff each cap with the crumb mixture. 3. Air fry in the zone 1 air fryer basket for 10 minutes. 4. Serve hot.
Make the Simple Zucchini Crisps (zone 2 basket): 1. Preheat the zone 2 air fryer basket to 392°F (200°C). Spritz the zone 2 air fryer basket with cooking spray. 2. Put the zucchini rounds in the zone 2 air fryer basket, spreading them out as much as possible. Top with a sprinkle of garlic granules, sea salt, and black pepper (if desired). Spritz the zucchini rounds with cooking spray. 3. Roast for 14 minutes, flipping the zucchini rounds halfway through, or until the zucchini rounds are crisp-tender. 4. Let them rest for 5 minutes and serve.

Corn Croquettes

Prep time: 10 minutes | Cook time: 12 to 14 minutes | Serves 4

½ cup leftover mashed potatoes
2 cups corn kernels (if frozen, thawed, and well drained)
¼ teaspoon onion powder
⅛ teaspoon ground black pepper
¼ teaspoon salt
½ cup panko bread crumbs
Oil for misting or cooking spray

1. Place the potatoes and half the corn in food processor and pulse until corn is well chopped. 2. Transfer mixture to large bowl and stir in remaining corn, onion powder, pepper and salt. 3. Shape mixture into 16 balls. 4. Roll balls in panko crumbs, mist with oil or cooking spray, and place in the two air fryer baskets. 5. Air fry at 360°F (182°C) for 12 to 14 minutes, until golden brown and crispy.

Crispy Green Beans and Lush Vegetable Salad

Prep time: 20 minutes | Cook time: 10 minutes | Serves 8

Crispy Green Beans:
2 teaspoons olive oil
½ pound (227 g) fresh green beans, ends trimmed
¼ teaspoon salt
¼ teaspoon ground black pepper
Lush Vegetable Salad:
6 plum tomatoes, halved
2 large red onions, sliced
4 long red pepper, sliced
2 yellow pepper, sliced
6 cloves garlic, crushed
1 tablespoon extra-virgin olive oil
1 teaspoon paprika
½ lemon, juiced
Salt and ground black pepper, to taste
1 tablespoon baby capers

Make the Crispy Green Beans (zone 1 basket): 1. In a large bowl, drizzle olive oil over green beans and sprinkle with salt and pepper. 2. Place green beans into the ungreased zone 1 air fryer basket. Adjust the temperature to 350°F (177°C) and set the timer for 8 minutes, shaking the basket two times during cooking. Green beans will be dark golden and crispy at the edges when done. Serve warm. Make the Lush Vegetable Salad (zone 2 basket): 1. Preheat the zone 2 air fryer basket to 420°F (216°C). 2. Put the tomatoes, onions, peppers, and garlic in a large bowl and cover with the extra-virgin olive oil, paprika, and lemon juice. Sprinkle with salt and pepper as desired. 3. Line the inside of the zone 2 air fryer basket with aluminum foil. Put the vegetables inside and air fry for 10 minutes, ensuring the edges turn brown. 4. Serve in a salad bowl with the baby capers.

Garlic Herb Radishes and Ratatouille

Prep time: 25 minutes | Cook time: 20 minutes | Serves 6-7

Garlic Herb Radishes:
1 pound (454 g) radishes
2 tablespoons unsalted butter, melted
½ teaspoon garlic powder
½ teaspoon dried parsley
¼ teaspoon dried oregano
¼ teaspoon ground black pepper
Ratatouille:
2 cups ¾-inch cubed peeled eggplant
1 small red, yellow, or orange bell pepper, stemmed, seeded, and diced
1 cup cherry tomatoes
6 to 8 cloves garlic, peeled and halved lengthwise
3 tablespoons olive oil
1 teaspoon dried oregano
½ teaspoon dried thyme
1 teaspoon kosher salt
½ teaspoon black pepper

Make the Garlic Herb Radishes (zone 1 basket): 1. Remove roots from radishes and cut into quarters. 2. In a small bowl, add butter and seasonings. Toss the radishes in the herb butter and place into the zone 1 air fryer basket. 3. Adjust the temperature to 350°F (177°C) and set the timer for 10 minutes. 4. Halfway through the cooking time, toss the radishes in the zone 1 air fryer basket. Continue cooking until edges begin to turn brown. 5. Serve warm. Make the Ratatouille (zone 2 basket): 1. In a medium bowl, combine the eggplant, bell pepper, tomatoes, garlic, oil, oregano, thyme, salt, and pepper. Toss to combine. 2. Place the vegetables in the zone 2 air fryer basket. Set the air fryer to 400°F (204°C) for 20 minutes, or until the vegetables are crisp-tender.

Parmesan and Herb Sweet Potatoes

Prep time: 10 minutes | Cook time: 18 minutes | Serves 4

2 large sweet potatoes, peeled and cubed
¼ cup olive oil
1 teaspoon dried rosemary
½ teaspoon salt
2 tablespoons shredded Parmesan

1. Preheat the zone 1 air fryer basket to 360°F (182°C). 2. In a large bowl, toss the sweet potatoes with the olive oil, rosemary, and salt. 3. Pour the potatoes into the zone 1 air fryer basket and roast for 10 minutes, then stir the potatoes and sprinkle the Parmesan over the top. Continue roasting for 8 minutes more. 4. Serve hot and enjoy.

Fried Zucchini Salad

Prep time: 10 minutes | Cook time: 5 to 7 minutes | Serves 4

2 medium zucchini, thinly sliced
5 tablespoons olive oil, divided
¼ cup chopped fresh parsley
2 tablespoons chopped fresh mint
Zest and juice of ½ lemon
1 clove garlic, minced
¼ cup crumbled feta cheese
Freshly ground black pepper, to taste

1. Preheat the air fryer to 400°F (204°C). 2. In a large bowl, toss the zucchini slices with 1 tablespoon of the olive oil. 3. Arrange the zucchini slices in an even layer in the two air fryer baskets. Pausing halfway through the cooking time to shake the baskets, air fry for 5 to 7 minutes until soft and lightly browned on each side. 4. Meanwhile, in a small bowl, combine the remaining 4 tablespoons olive oil, parsley, mint, lemon zest, lemon juice, and garlic. 5. Arrange the zucchini on a plate and drizzle with the dressing. Sprinkle the feta and black pepper on top. Serve warm or at room temperature.

Radish Chips

Prep time: 10 minutes | Cook time: 5 minutes | Serves 4

2 cups water
1 pound (454 g) radishes
¼ teaspoon onion powder
¼ teaspoon paprika
½ teaspoon garlic powder
2 tablespoons coconut oil, melted

1. Place water in a medium saucepan and bring to a boil on stovetop. 2. Remove the top and bottom from each radish, then use a mandoline to slice each radish thin and uniformly. You may also use the slicing blade in the food processor for this step. 3. Place the radish slices into the boiling water for 5 minutes or until translucent. Remove them from the water and place them into a clean kitchen towel to absorb excess moisture. 4. Toss the radish chips in a large bowl with remaining ingredients until fully coated in oil and seasoning. Place radish chips into the two air fryer baskets. 5. Adjust the temperature to 320°F (160°C) and air fry for 5 minutes. 6. Shake the basket two or three times during the cooking time. Serve warm.

Saltine Wax Beans

Prep time: 10 minutes | Cook time: 7 minutes | Serves 4

½ cup flour
1 teaspoon smoky chipotle powder
½ teaspoon ground black pepper
1 teaspoon sea salt flakes

2 eggs, beaten
½ cup crushed saltines
10 ounces (283 g) wax beans
Cooking spray

1. Preheat the zone 1 air fryer basket to 360°F (182°C). 2. Combine the flour, chipotle powder, black pepper, and salt in a bowl. Put the eggs in a second bowl. Put the crushed saltines in a third bowl. 3. Wash the beans with cold water and discard any tough strings. 4. Coat the beans with the flour mixture, before dipping them into the beaten egg. Cover them with the crushed saltines. 5. Spritz the beans with cooking spray. 6. Air fry for 4 minutes. Give the zone 1 air fryer basket a good shake and continue to air fry for 3 minutes. Serve hot.

Indian Eggplant Bharta

Prep time: 15 minutes | Cook time: 20 minutes | Serves 4

1 medium eggplant
2 tablespoons vegetable oil
½ cup finely minced onion
½ cup finely chopped fresh tomato

2 tablespoons fresh lemon juice
2 tablespoons chopped fresh cilantro
½ teaspoon kosher salt
⅛ teaspoon cayenne pepper

1. Rub the eggplant all over with the vegetable oil. Place the eggplant in the zone 1 air fryer basket. Set the air fryer to 400°F (204°C) for 20 minutes, or until the eggplant skin is blistered and charred. 2. Transfer the eggplant to a resealable plastic bag, seal, and set aside for 15 to 20 minutes (the eggplant will finish cooking in the residual heat trapped in the bag). 3. Transfer the eggplant to a large bowl. Peel off and discard the charred skin. Roughly mash the eggplant flesh. Add the onion, tomato, lemon juice, cilantro, salt, and cayenne. Stir to combine.

Chapter 4 Fish and Seafood

Chapter 4 Fish and Seafood

Tuna and Fruit Kebabs and Parmesan Mackerel with Coriander

Prep time: 25 minutes | Cook time: 8 to 12 minutes | Serves 6

Tuna and Fruit Kebabs:
1 pound (454 g) tuna steaks, cut into 1-inch cubes
½ cup canned pineapple chunks, drained, juice reserved
½ cup large red grapes
1 tablespoon honey
2 teaspoons grated fresh ginger
1 teaspoon olive oil
Pinch cayenne pepper
Parmesan Mackerel with Coriander:
12 ounces (340 g) mackerel fillet
2 ounces (57 g) Parmesan, grated
1 teaspoon ground coriander
1 tablespoon olive oil

Make the Tuna and Fruit Kebabs (zone 1 basket): 1. Thread the tuna, pineapple, and grapes on 8 bamboo or 4 metal skewers that fit in the air fryer. 2. In a small bowl, whisk the honey, 1 tablespoon of reserved pineapple juice, the ginger, olive oil, and cayenne. Brush this mixture over the kebabs. Let them stand for 10 minutes. 3. Air fry the kebabs in the zone 1 air fryer basket at 370°F (188°C) for 8 to 12 minutes, or until the tuna reaches an internal temperature of at least 145°F (63°C) on a meat thermometer, and the fruit is tender and glazed, brushing once with the remaining sauce. Discard any remaining marinade. Serve immediately.
Make the Parmesan Mackerel with Coriander (zone 2 basket): 1. Sprinkle the mackerel fillet with olive oil and put it in the zone 2 air fryer basket. 2. Top the fish with ground coriander and Parmesan. 3. Cook the fish at 390°F (199°C) for 7 minutes.

Crustless Shrimp Quiche and Shrimp with Swiss Chard

Prep time: 25 minutes | Cook time: 20 minutes | Serves 6

Crustless Shrimp Quiche:
Vegetable oil
4 large eggs
½ cup half-and-half
4 ounces (113 g) raw shrimp, chopped (about 1 cup)
1 cup shredded Parmesan or Swiss cheese
¼ cup chopped scallions
1 teaspoon sweet smoked paprika
1 teaspoon herbes de Provence
1 teaspoon black pepper
½ to 1 teaspoon kosher salt
Shrimp with Swiss Chard:
1 pound (454 g) shrimp, peeled and deveined
½ teaspoon smoked paprika
½ cup Swiss chard, chopped
2 tablespoons apple cider vinegar
1 tablespoon coconut oil
¼ cup heavy cream

Make the Crustless Shrimp Quiche: 1. Generously grease a baking pan with vegetable oil. (Be sure to grease the pan well, the proteins in eggs stick something fierce. Alternatively, line the bottom of the pan with parchment paper cut to fit and spray the parchment and sides of the pan generously with vegetable oil spray.) 2. In a large bowl, beat together the eggs and half-and-half. Add the shrimp, ¾ cup of the cheese, the scallions, paprika, herbes de Provence, pepper, and salt. Stir with a fork to thoroughly combine. Pour the egg mixture into the prepared pan. 3. Place the pan in the zone 1 air fryer basket. Set the air fryer to 300°F (149°C) for 20 minutes. After 17 minutes, sprinkle the remaining ¼ cup cheese on top and cook for the remaining 3 minutes, or until the cheese has melted, the eggs are set, and a toothpick inserted into the center comes out clean. 4. Serve the quiche warm or at room temperature.
Make the Shrimp with Swiss Chard: 1. Mix shrimps with smoked paprika and apple cider vinegar. 2. Put the shrimps in the zone 2 air fryer basket and add coconut oil. 3. Cook the shrimps at 350°F (177°C) for 10 minutes. 4. Then mix cooked shrimps with remaining ingredients and carefully mix.

Cilantro Lime Baked Salmon and Almond Pesto Salmon

Prep time: 15 minutes | Cook time: 12 minutes | Serves 4

Cilantro Lime Baked Salmon:
2 (3-ounce / 85-g) salmon fillets, skin removed
1 tablespoon salted butter, melted
1 teaspoon chili powder
½ teaspoon finely minced garlic
¼ cup sliced pickled jalapeños
½ medium lime, juiced
2 tablespoons chopped cilantro
Almond Pesto Salmon:
¼ cup pesto
¼ cup sliced almonds, roughly chopped
2 (1½-inch-thick) salmon fillets (about 4 ounces / 113 g each)
2 tablespoons unsalted butter, melted

Make the Cilantro Lime Baked Salmon (zone 1 basket): 1. Place salmon fillets into a round baking pan. Brush each with butter and sprinkle with chili powder and garlic. 2. Place jalapeño slices on top and around salmon. Pour half of the lime juice over the salmon and cover with foil. Place pan into the zone 1 air fryer basket. 3. Adjust the temperature to 370°F (188°C) and bake for 12 minutes. 4. When fully cooked, salmon should flake easily with a fork and reach an internal temperature of at least 145°F (63°C). 5. To serve, spritz with remaining lime juice and garnish with cilantro.
Make the Almond Pesto Salmon (zone 2 basket): 1. In a small bowl, mix pesto and almonds. Set aside. 2. Place fillets into a round baking dish. 3. Brush each fillet with butter and place half of the pesto mixture on the top of each fillet. Place dish into the zone 2 air fryer basket. 4. Adjust the temperature to 390°F (199°C) and set the timer for 12 minutes. 5. Salmon will easily flake when fully cooked and reach an internal temperature of at least 145°F (63°C). Serve warm.

Sweet Tilapia Fillets

Prep time: 5 minutes | Cook time: 14 minutes | Serves 4

2 tablespoons erythritol
1 tablespoon apple cider vinegar
4 tilapia fillets, boneless
1 teaspoon olive oil

1. Mix apple cider vinegar with olive oil and erythritol. 2. Then rub the tilapia fillets with the sweet mixture and put in the two air fryer baskets in one layer. Cook the fish at 360ºF (182ºC) for 7 minutes per side.

Shrimp Bake

Prep time: 15 minutes | Cook time: 5 minutes | Serves 4

14 ounces (397 g) shrimp, peeled
1 egg, beaten
½ cup coconut milk
1 cup Cheddar cheese, shredded
½ teaspoon coconut oil
1 teaspoon ground coriander

1. In the mixing bowl, mix shrimps with egg, coconut milk, Cheddar cheese, coconut oil, and ground coriander. 2. Then put the mixture in the baking ramekins and put in the two air fryer baskets. 3. Cook the shrimps at 400ºF (204ºC) for 5 minutes.

Cod with Jalapeño

Prep time: 5 minutes | Cook time: 14 minutes | Serves 4

4 cod fillets, boneless
1 jalapeño, minced
1 tablespoon avocado oil
½ teaspoon minced garlic

1. In the shallow bowl, mix minced jalapeño, avocado oil, and minced garlic. 2. Put the cod fillets in the two air fryer baskets in one layer and top with minced jalapeño mixture. 3. Cook the fish at 365ºF (185ºC) for 7 minutes per side.

Tandoori Shrimp

Prep time: 25 minutes | Cook time: 6 minutes | Serves 4

1 pound (454 g) jumbo raw shrimp (21 to 25 count), peeled and deveined
1 tablespoon minced fresh ginger
3 cloves garlic, minced
¼ cup chopped fresh cilantro or parsley, plus more for garnish
1 teaspoon ground turmeric
1 teaspoon garam masala
1 teaspoon smoked paprika
1 teaspoon kosher salt
½ to 1 teaspoon cayenne pepper
2 tablespoons olive oil (for Paleo) or melted ghee
2 teaspoons fresh lemon juice

1. In a large bowl, combine the shrimp, ginger, garlic, cilantro, turmeric, garam masala, paprika, salt, and cayenne. Toss well to coat. Add the oil or ghee and toss again. Marinate at room temperature for 15 minutes, or cover and refrigerate for up to 8 hours. 2. Place the shrimp in a single layer in the two air fryer baskets. Set the air fryer to 325ºF (163ºC) for 6 minutes. Transfer the shrimp to a serving platter. Cover and let the shrimp finish cooking in the residual heat, about 5 minutes. 3. Sprinkle the shrimp with the lemon juice and toss to coat. Garnish with additional cilantro and serve.

Garlic Lemon Scallops

Prep time: 5 minutes | Cook time: 10 minutes | Serves 4

4 tablespoons salted butter, melted
4 teaspoons peeled and finely minced garlic
½ small lemon, zested and juiced
8 (1-ounce / 28-g) sea scallops, cleaned and patted dry
¼ teaspoon salt
¼ teaspoon ground black pepper

1. In a small bowl, mix butter, garlic, lemon zest, and lemon juice. Place scallops in an ungreased round nonstick baking dish. Pour butter mixture over scallops, then sprinkle with salt and pepper. 2. Place dish into the zone 1 air fryer basket. Adjust the temperature to 360ºF (182ºC) and bake for 10 minutes. Scallops will be opaque and firm, and have an internal temperature of 135ºF (57ºC) when done. Serve warm.

South Indian Fried Fish

Prep time: 20 minutes | Cook time: 8 minutes | Serves 4

2 tablespoons olive oil
2 tablespoons fresh lime or lemon juice
1 teaspoon minced fresh ginger
1 clove garlic, minced
1 teaspoon ground turmeric
½ teaspoon kosher salt
¼ to ½ teaspoon cayenne pepper
1 pound (454 g) tilapia fillets (2 to 3 fillets)
Olive oil spray
Lime or lemon wedges (optional)

1. In a large bowl, combine the oil, lime juice, ginger, garlic, turmeric, salt, and cayenne. Stir until well combined; set aside. 2. Cut each tilapia fillet into three or four equal-size pieces. Add the fish to the bowl and gently mix until all of the fish is coated in the marinade. Marinate for 10 to 15 minutes at room temperature. (Don't marinate any longer or the acid in the lime juice will "cook" the fish.) 3. Spray the zone 1 air fryer basket with olive oil spray. Place the fish in the zone 1 basket and spray the fish. Set the temperature to 325ºF (163ºC) for 3 minutes to partially cook the fish. Set the temperature to 400ºF (204ºC) for 5 minutes to finish cooking and crisp up the fish. (Thinner pieces of fish will cook faster so you may want to check at the 3-minute mark of the second cooking time and remove those that are cooked through, and then add them back toward the end of the second cooking time to crisp.) 4. Carefully remove the fish from the basket. Serve hot, with lemon wedges if desired.

Blackened Fish

Prep time: 15 minutes | Cook time: 8 minutes | Serves 4

1 large egg, beaten
Blackened seasoning, as needed
2 tablespoons light brown sugar
4 (4-ounce / 113-g) tilapia fillets
Cooking spray

1. In a shallow bowl, place the beaten egg. In a second shallow bowl, stir together the Blackened seasoning and the brown sugar. 2. One at a time, dip the fish fillets in the egg, then the brown sugar mixture, coating thoroughly. 3. Preheat the air fryer to 300°F (149°C). Line the two air fryer baskets with parchment paper. 4. Place the coated fish on the parchment and spritz with oil. 5. Bake for 4 minutes. Flip the fish, spritz it with oil, and bake for 4 to 6 minutes more until the fish is white inside and flakes easily with a fork. 6. Serve immediately.

Tuna Patty Sliders

Prep time: 15 minutes | Cook time: 10 to 15 minutes | Serves 4

3 (5-ounce / 142-g) cans tuna, packed in water
⅔ cup whole-wheat panko bread crumbs
⅓ cup shredded Parmesan cheese
1 tablespoon sriracha
¾ teaspoon black pepper
10 whole-wheat slider buns
Cooking spray

1. Preheat the air fryer to 350°F (177°C). 2. Spray the two air fryer baskets lightly with cooking spray. 3. In a medium bowl combine the tuna, bread crumbs, Parmesan cheese, sriracha, and black pepper and stir to combine. 4. Form the mixture into 10 patties. 5. Place the patties in the two air fryer baskets in a single layer. Spray the patties lightly with cooking spray. 6. Air fry for 6 to 8 minutes. Turn the patties over and lightly spray with cooking spray. Air fry until golden brown and crisp, another 4 to 7 more minutes. Serve warm.

Air Fried Spring Rolls

Prep time: 10 minutes | Cook time: 17 to 22 minutes | Serves 4

2 teaspoons minced garlic
2 cups finely sliced cabbage
1 cup matchstick cut carrots
2 (4-ounce / 113-g) cans tiny shrimp, drained
4 teaspoons soy sauce
Salt and freshly ground black pepper, to taste
16 square spring roll wrappers
Cooking spray

1. Preheat the air fryer to 370°F (188°C). 2. Spray the two air fryer baskets lightly with cooking spray. Spray a medium sauté pan with cooking spray. 3. Add the garlic to the sauté pan and cook over medium heat until fragrant, 30 to 45 seconds. Add the cabbage and carrots and sauté until the vegetables are slightly tender, about 5 minutes. 4. Add the shrimp and soy sauce and season with salt and pepper, then stir to combine. Sauté until the moisture has evaporated, 2 more minutes. Set aside to cool. 5. Place a spring roll wrapper on a work surface so it looks like a diamond. Place 1 tablespoon of the shrimp mixture on the lower end of the wrapper. 6. Roll the wrapper away from you halfway, then fold in the right and left sides, like an envelope. Continue to roll to the very end, using a little water to seal the edge. Repeat with the remaining wrappers and filling. 7. Place the spring rolls in the two air fryer baskets in a single layer, leaving room between each roll. Lightly spray with cooking spray. 8. Air fry for 5 minutes. Turn the rolls over, lightly spray with cooking spray, and air fry until heated through and the rolls start to brown, 5 to 10 more minutes. Cool for 5 minutes before serving.

Lemony Shrimp and Zucchini

Prep time: 15 minutes | Cook time: 7 to 8 minutes | Serves 4

1¼ pounds (567 g) extra-large raw shrimp, peeled and deveined
2 medium zucchini (about 8 ounces / 227 g each), halved lengthwise and cut into ½-inch-thick slices
1½ tablespoons olive oil
½ teaspoon garlic salt
1½ teaspoons dried oregano
⅛ teaspoon crushed red pepper flakes (optional)
Juice of ½ lemon
1 tablespoon chopped fresh mint
1 tablespoon chopped fresh dill

1. Preheat the air fryer to 350°F (177°C). 2. In a large bowl, combine the shrimp, zucchini, oil, garlic salt, oregano, and pepper flakes (if using) and toss to coat. 3. Arrange a single layer of the shrimp and zucchini in the two air fryer baskets. Air fry for 7 to 8 minutes, shaking the baskets halfway, until the zucchini is golden and the shrimp are cooked through. 4. Transfer to a serving dish and tent with foil while you air fry the remaining shrimp and zucchini. 5. Top with the lemon juice, mint, and dill and serve.

Cod with Creamy Mustard Sauce

Prep time: 10 minutes | Cook time: 10 minutes | Serves 4

Fish:
Oil, for spraying
1 pound (454 g) cod fillets
2 tablespoons olive oil
1 tablespoon lemon juice
1 teaspoon salt
½ teaspoon freshly ground black pepper
Mustard Sauce:
½ cup heavy cream
3 tablespoons Dijon mustard
1 tablespoon unsalted butter
1 teaspoon salt

Make the Fish 1. Line the two air fryer baskets with parchment and spray lightly with oil. 2. Rub the cod with the olive oil and lemon juice. Season with the salt and black pepper. 3. Place the cod in the prepared baskets. 4. Roast at 350°F (177°C) for 5 minutes. Increase the temperature to 400°F (204°C) and cook for another 5 minutes, until flaky and the internal temperature reaches 145°F (63°C). Make the Mustard Sauce 5. In a small saucepan, mix together the heavy cream, mustard, butter, and salt and bring to a simmer over low heat. Cook for 3 to 4 minutes, or until the sauce starts to thicken. 6. Transfer the cod to a serving plate and drizzle with the mustard sauce. Serve immediately.

Sea Bass with Roasted Root Vegetables

Prep time: 10 minutes | Cook time: 15 minutes | Serves 4

1 carrot, diced small	4 sea bass fillets
1 parsnip, diced small	½ teaspoon onion powder
1 rutabaga, diced small	2 garlic cloves, minced
¼ cup olive oil	1 lemon, sliced, plus additional wedges for serving
1 teaspoon salt, divided	

1. Preheat the air fryer to 380°F(193°C). 2. In a small bowl, toss the carrot, parsnip, and rutabaga with olive oil and 1 teaspoon salt. 3. Lightly season the sea bass with the remaining 1 teaspoon of salt and the onion powder, then place it into the two air fryer baskets in a single layer. 4. Spread the garlic over the top of each fillet, then cover with lemon slices. 5. Pour the prepared vegetables into the basket around and on top of the fish. Roast for 15 minutes. 6. Serve with additional lemon wedges if desired.

Catfish Bites

Prep time: 15 minutes | Cook time: 20 minutes | Serves 4

Oil, for spraying	½ cup cornmeal
1 pound (454 g) catfish fillets, cut into 2-inch pieces	¼ cup all-purpose flour
1 cup buttermilk	2 teaspoons Creole seasoning
	½ cup yellow mustard

1. Line the two air fryer baskets with parchment and spray lightly with oil. 2. Place the catfish pieces and buttermilk in a zip-top plastic bag, seal, and refrigerate for about 10 minutes. 3. In a shallow bowl, mix together the cornmeal, flour, and Creole seasoning. 4. Remove the catfish from the bag and pat dry with a paper towel. 5. Spread the mustard on all sides of the catfish, then dip them in the cornmeal mixture until evenly coated. 6. Place the catfish in the two prepared baskets. Spray lightly with oil. 7. Air fry at 400°F (204°C) for 10 minutes, flip carefully, spray with oil, and cook for another 10 minutes. Serve immediately.

Shrimp and Cherry Tomato Kebabs

Prep time: 15 minutes | Cook time: 5 minutes | Serves 4

1½ pounds (680 g) jumbo shrimp, cleaned, shelled and deveined	1 teaspoon dried parsley flakes
1 pound (454 g) cherry tomatoes	½ teaspoon dried basil
2 tablespoons butter, melted	½ teaspoon dried oregano
1 tablespoons Sriracha sauce	½ teaspoon mustard seeds
Sea salt and ground black pepper, to taste	½ teaspoon marjoram
	Special Equipment:
	4 to 6 wooden skewers, soaked in water for 30 minutes

1. Preheat the air fryer to 400°F (204°C). 2. Put all the ingredients in a large bowl and toss to coat well. 3. Make the kebabs: Thread, alternating jumbo shrimp and cherry tomatoes, onto the wooden skewers that fit into the air fryer. 4. Arrange the kebabs in the two air fryer baskets. 5. Air fry for 5 minutes, or until the shrimp are pink and the cherry tomatoes are softened. Repeat with the remaining kebabs. Let the shrimp and cherry tomato kebabs cool for 5 minutes and serve hot.

Balsamic Tilapia

Prep time: 5 minutes | Cook time: 15 minutes | Serves 4

4 tilapia fillets, boneless	1 teaspoon avocado oil
2 tablespoons balsamic vinegar	1 teaspoon dried basil

1. Sprinkle the tilapia fillets with balsamic vinegar, avocado oil, and dried basil. 2. Then put the fillets in the two air fryer baskets and cook at 365°F (185°C) for 15 minutes.

Paprika Crab Burgers

Prep time: 30 minutes | Cook time: 14 minutes | Serves 3

2 eggs, beaten	chopped
1 shallot, chopped	10 ounces (283 g) crab meat
2 garlic cloves, crushed	1 teaspoon smoked paprika
1 tablespoon olive oil	½ teaspoon ground black pepper
1 teaspoon yellow mustard	Sea salt, to taste
1 teaspoon fresh cilantro,	¾ cup Parmesan cheese

1. In a mixing bowl, thoroughly combine the eggs, shallot, garlic, olive oil, mustard, cilantro, crab meat, paprika, black pepper, and salt. Mix until well combined. 2. Shape the mixture into 6 patties. Roll the crab patties over grated Parmesan cheese, coating well on all sides. Place in your refrigerator for 2 hours. 3. Spritz the crab patties with cooking oil on both sides. Cook in the preheated air fryer at 360°F (182°C) for 14 minutes. Serve on dinner rolls if desired. Bon appétit!

Crispy Herbed Salmon

Prep time: 5 minutes | Cook time: 9 to 12 minutes | Serves 4

4 (6-ounce / 170-g) skinless salmon fillets	½ teaspoon dried basil
3 tablespoons honey mustard	¼ cup panko bread crumbs
½ teaspoon dried thyme	⅓ cup crushed potato chips
	2 tablespoons olive oil

1. Place the salmon on a plate. In a small bowl, combine the mustard, thyme, and basil, and spread evenly over the salmon. 2. In another small bowl, combine the bread crumbs and potato chips and mix well. Drizzle in the olive oil and mix until combined. 3. Place the salmon in the two air fryer baskets and gently but firmly press the bread crumb mixture onto the top of each fillet. 4. Bake at 320°F (160°C) for 9 to 12 minutes or until the salmon reaches at least 145°F (63°C) on a meat thermometer and the topping is browned and crisp.

Honey-Glazed Salmon

Prep time: 5 minutes | Cook time: 12 minutes | Serves 4

¼ cup raw honey
4 garlic cloves, minced
1 tablespoon olive oil
½ teaspoon salt
Olive oil cooking spray
4 (1½-inch-thick) salmon fillets

1. Preheat the air fryer to 380°F(193°C). 2. In a small bowl, mix together the honey, garlic, olive oil, and salt. 3. Spray the bottom of the two air fryer baskets with olive oil cooking spray, and place the salmon in a single layer on the bottom of the air fryer baskets. 4. Brush the top of each fillet with the honey-garlic mixture, and roast for 10 to 12 minutes, or until the internal temperature reaches 145°F(63°C).

BBQ Shrimp with Creole Butter Sauce and Fish Fillets with Lemon-Dill Sauce

Prep time: 15 minutes | Cook time: 12 to 15 minutes | Serves 8

BBQ Shrimp with Creole Butter Sauce:
6 tablespoons unsalted butter
⅓ cup Worcestershire sauce
3 cloves garlic, minced
Juice of 1 lemon
1 teaspoon paprika
1 teaspoon Creole seasoning
1½ pounds (680 g) large uncooked shrimp, peeled and deveined
2 tablespoons fresh parsley
Fish Fillets with Lemon-Dill Sauce:
1 pound (454 g) snapper, grouper, or salmon fillets
Sea salt and freshly ground black pepper, to taste
1 tablespoon avocado oil
¼ cup sour cream
¼ cup sugar-free mayonnaise
2 tablespoons fresh dill, chopped, plus more for garnish
1 tablespoon freshly squeezed lemon juice
½ teaspoon grated lemon zest

Make the BBQ Shrimp with Creole Butter Sauce (zone 1 basket): 1. Preheat the zone 1 air fryer basket to 370°F (188°C). 2. In a large microwave-safe bowl, combine the butter, Worcestershire, and garlic. Microwave on high for 1 to 2 minutes until the butter is melted. Stir in the lemon juice, paprika, and Creole seasoning. Add the shrimp and toss until thoroughly coated. 3. Transfer the mixture to a casserole dish or pan that fits in your air fryer. Pausing halfway through the cooking time to turn the shrimp, air fry for 12 to 15 minutes, until the shrimp are cooked through. Top with the parsley just before serving.
Make the Fish Fillets with Lemon-Dill Sauce (zone 2 basket): 1. Pat the fish dry with paper towels and season well with salt and pepper. Brush with the avocado oil. 2. Set the zone 2 air fryer basket to 400°F (204°C). Place the fillets in the zone 2 air fryer basket and air fry for 1 minute. 3. Lower the temperature to 325°F (163°C) and continue cooking for 5 minutes. Flip the fish and cook for 1 minute more or until an instant-read thermometer reads 145°F (63°C). (If using salmon, cook it to 125°F / 52°C for medium-rare.) 4. While the fish is cooking, make the sauce by combining the sour cream, mayonnaise, dill, lemon juice, and lemon zest in a medium bowl. Season with salt and pepper and stir until combined. Refrigerate until ready to serve. 5. Serve the fish with the sauce, garnished with the remaining dill.

Snapper with Fruit

Prep time: 15 minutes | Cook time: 9 to 13 minutes | Serves 4

4 (4-ounce / 113-g) red snapper fillets
2 teaspoons olive oil
3 nectarines, halved and pitted
3 plums, halved and pitted
1 cup red grapes
1 tablespoon freshly squeezed lemon juice
1 tablespoon honey
½ teaspoon dried thyme

1. Put the red snapper in the two air fryer baskets and drizzle with the olive oil. Air fry at 390°F (199°C) for 4 minutes. 2. Remove the basket and add the nectarines and plums. Scatter the grapes over all. 3. Drizzle with the lemon juice and honey and sprinkle with the thyme. 4. Return the baskets to the air fryer and air fry for 5 to 9 minutes more, or until the fish flakes when tested with a fork and the fruit is tender. Serve immediately.

Fish Taco Bowl

Prep time: 10 minutes | Cook time: 12 minutes | Serves 4

½ teaspoon salt
¼ teaspoon garlic powder
¼ teaspoon ground cumin
4 (4-ounce / 113-g) cod fillets
4 cups finely shredded green cabbage
⅓ cup mayonnaise
¼ teaspoon ground black pepper
¼ cup chopped pickled jalapeños

1. Sprinkle salt, garlic powder, and cumin over cod and place into two ungreased air fryer baskets. Adjust the temperature to 350°F (177°C) and air fry for 12 minutes, turning fillets halfway through cooking. Cod will flake easily and have an internal temperature of at least 145°F (63°C) when done. 2. In a large bowl, toss cabbage with mayonnaise, pepper, and jalapeños until fully coated. Serve cod warm over cabbage slaw on four medium plates.

Parmesan Lobster Tails

Prep time: 5 minutes | Cook time: 7 minutes | Serves 4

4 (4-ounce / 113-g) lobster tails
2 tablespoons salted butter, melted
1½ teaspoons Cajun seasoning, divided
¼ teaspoon salt
¼ teaspoon ground black pepper
¼ cup grated Parmesan cheese
½ ounce (14 g) plain pork rinds, finely crushed

1. Cut lobster tails open carefully with a pair of scissors and gently pull meat away from shells, resting meat on top of shells. 2. Brush lobster meat with butter and sprinkle with 1 teaspoon Cajun seasoning, ¼ teaspoon per tail. 3. In a small bowl, mix remaining Cajun seasoning, salt, pepper, Parmesan, and pork rinds. Gently press ¼ mixture onto meat on each lobster tail. 4. Carefully place tails into two ungreased air fryer baskets. Adjust the temperature to 400°F (204°C) and air fry for 7 minutes. Lobster tails will be crispy and golden on top and have an internal temperature of at least 145°F (63°C) when done. Serve warm.

Confetti Salmon Burgers

Prep time: 10 minutes | Cook time: 12 minutes | Serves 4

14 ounces (397 g) cooked fresh or canned salmon, flaked with a fork
¼ cup minced scallion, white and light green parts only
¼ cup minced red bell pepper
¼ cup minced celery
2 small lemons
1 teaspoon crab boil seasoning such as Old Bay
½ teaspoon kosher salt
½ teaspoon black pepper
1 egg, beaten
½ cup fresh bread crumbs
Vegetable oil, for spraying

1. In a large bowl, combine the salmon, vegetables, the zest and juice of 1 of the lemons, crab boil seasoning, salt, and pepper. Add the egg and bread crumbs and stir to combine. Form the mixture into 4 patties weighing approximately 5 ounces (142 g) each. Chill until firm, about 15 minutes. 2. Preheat the air fryer to 400°F (204°C). 3. Spray the salmon patties with oil on all sides and spray the two air fryer baskets to prevent sticking. Air fry for 12 minutes, flipping halfway through, until the burgers are browned and cooked through. Cut the remaining lemon into 4 wedges and serve with the burgers.

Spinach Scallops and Lemon-Tarragon Fish en Papillote

Prep time: 15 minutes | Cook time: 15 minutes | Serves 4

Spinach Scallops:
Vegetable oil spray
1 (10-ounce / 283-g) package frozen spinach, thawed and drained
8 jumbo sea scallops
Kosher salt and black pepper, to taste
¾ cup heavy cream
1 tablespoon tomato paste
1 tablespoon chopped fresh basil
1 teaspoon minced garlic
Lemon-Tarragon Fish en Papillote:
2 tablespoons salted butter, melted
1 tablespoon fresh lemon juice
½ teaspoon dried tarragon, crushed, or 2 sprigs fresh tarragon
1 teaspoon kosher salt
½ cup julienned carrots
½ cup julienned fennel, or ¼ cup julienned celery
½ cup thinly sliced red bell pepper
2 (6-ounce / 170-g) cod fillets, thawed if frozen
Vegetable oil spray
½ teaspoon black pepper

Make the Spinach Scallops (zone 1 basket): 1. Spray a baking pan with vegetable oil spray. Spread the thawed spinach in an even layer in the bottom of the pan. 2. Spray both sides of the scallops with vegetable oil spray. Season lightly with salt and pepper. Arrange the scallops on top of the spinach. 3. In a small bowl, whisk together the cream, tomato paste, basil, garlic, ½ teaspoon salt, and ½ teaspoon pepper. Pour the sauce over the scallops and spinach. 4. Place the pan in the zone 1 air fryer basket. Set the temperature to 350°F (177°C) for 10 minutes. Use a meat thermometer to ensure the scallops have an internal temperature of 135°F (57°C).
Make the Lemon-Tarragon Fish en Papillote (zone 2 basket): 1. In a medium bowl, combine the butter, lemon juice, tarragon, and ½ teaspoon of the salt. Whisk well until you get a creamy sauce. Add the carrots, fennel, and bell pepper and toss to combine; set aside. 2. Cut two squares of parchment each large enough to hold one fillet and half the vegetables. Spray the fillets with vegetable oil spray. Season both sides with the remaining ½ teaspoon salt and the black pepper. 3. Lay one fillet down on each parchment square. Top each with half the vegetables. Pour any remaining sauce over the vegetables. 4. Fold over the parchment paper and crimp the sides in small, tight folds to hold the fish, vegetables, and sauce securely inside the packet. Place the packets in the zone 2 air fryer basket. Set the temperature to 350°F (177°C) for 15 minutes. 5. Transfer each packet to a plate. Cut open with scissors just before serving (be careful, as the steam inside will be hot).

Garlicky Cod Fillets

Prep time: 10 minutes | Cook time: 10 to 12 minutes | Serves 4

1 teaspoon olive oil
4 cod fillets
¼ teaspoon fine sea salt
¼ teaspoon ground black pepper, or more to taste
1 teaspoon cayenne pepper
½ cup fresh Italian parsley, coarsely chopped
½ cup nondairy milk
1 Italian pepper, chopped
4 garlic cloves, minced
1 teaspoon dried basil
½ teaspoon dried oregano

1. Lightly coat the sides and bottom of two baking dishes with the olive oil. Set aside. 2. In a large bowl, sprinkle the fillets with salt, black pepper, and cayenne pepper. 3. In a food processor, pulse the remaining ingredients until smoothly puréed. 4. Add the purée to the bowl of fillets and toss to coat, then transfer to the prepared two baking dishes. 5. Preheat the air fryer to 380°F (193°C). 6. Put the baking dishes in the two air fryer baskets and bake for 10 to 12 minutes, or until the fish flakes when pressed lightly with a fork. 7. Remove from the baskets and serve warm.

Marinated Swordfish Skewers

Prep time: 30 minutes | Cook time: 6 to 8 minutes | Serves 4

1 pound (454 g) filleted swordfish
¼ cup avocado oil
2 tablespoons freshly squeezed lemon juice
1 tablespoon minced fresh parsley
2 teaspoons Dijon mustard
Sea salt and freshly ground black pepper, to taste
3 ounces (85 g) cherry tomatoes

1. Cut the fish into 1½-inch chunks, picking out any remaining bones. 2. In a large bowl, whisk together the oil, lemon juice, parsley, and Dijon mustard. Season to taste with salt and pepper. Add the fish and toss to coat the pieces. Cover and marinate the fish chunks in the refrigerator for 30 minutes. 3. Remove the fish from the marinade. Thread the fish and cherry tomatoes on 4 skewers, alternating as you go. 4. Set the air fryer to 400°F (204°C). Place the skewers in the two air fryer baskets and air fry for 3 minutes. Flip the skewers and cook for 3 to 5 minutes longer, until the fish is cooked through and an instant-read thermometer reads 140°F (60°C).

Shrimp Caesar Salad

Prep time: 30 minutes | Cook time: 4 to 6 minutes | Serves 4

12 ounces (340 g) fresh large shrimp, peeled and deveined
1 tablespoon plus 1 teaspoon freshly squeezed lemon juice, divided
4 tablespoons olive oil or avocado oil, divided
2 garlic cloves, minced, divided
¼ teaspoon sea salt, plus additional to season the marinade
¼ teaspoon freshly ground black pepper, plus additional to season the marinade
⅓ cup sugar-free mayonnaise
2 tablespoons freshly grated Parmesan cheese
1 teaspoon Dijon mustard
1 tinned anchovy, mashed
12 ounces (340 g) romaine hearts, torn

1. Place the shrimp in a large bowl. Add 1 tablespoon of lemon juice, 1 tablespoon of olive oil, and 1 minced garlic clove. Season with salt and pepper. Toss well and refrigerate for 15 minutes. 2. While the shrimp marinates, make the dressing: In a blender, combine the mayonnaise, Parmesan cheese, Dijon mustard, the remaining 1 teaspoon of lemon juice, the anchovy, the remaining minced garlic clove, ¼ teaspoon of salt, and ¼ teaspoon of pepper. Process until smooth. With the blender running, slowly stream in the remaining 3 tablespoons of oil. Transfer the mixture to a jar; seal and refrigerate until ready to serve. 3. Remove the shrimp from its marinade and place it in the two air fryer baskets in a single layer. Set the temperature to 400°F (204°C) and air fry for 2 minutes. Flip the shrimp and cook for 2 to 4 minutes more, until the flesh turns opaque. 4. Place the romaine in a large bowl and toss with the desired amount of dressing. Top with the shrimp and serve immediately.

Popcorn Crawfish and Tandoori-Spiced Salmon

Prep time: 25 minutes | Cook time: 28 minutes | Serves 6

Popcorn Crawfish:
½ cup flour, plus 2 tablespoons
½ teaspoon garlic powder
1½ teaspoons Old Bay Seasoning
½ teaspoon onion powder
½ cup beer, plus 2 tablespoons
1 (12-ounce / 340-g) package frozen crawfish tail meat, thawed and drained
Oil for misting or cooking spray
Coating:
1½ cups panko crumbs
1 teaspoon Old Bay Seasoning
½ teaspoon ground black pepper
Tandoori-Spiced Salmon:
1 pound (454 g) fingerling potatoes
2 tablespoons vegetable oil, divided
Kosher salt and freshly ground black pepper, to taste
1 teaspoon ground turmeric
1 teaspoon ground cumin
1 teaspoon ground ginger
½ teaspoon smoked paprika
¼ teaspoon cayenne pepper
2 (6-ounce / 170-g) skin-on salmon fillets

Make the Popcorn Crawfish (zone 1 basket): 1. In a large bowl, mix together the flour, garlic powder, Old Bay Seasoning, and onion powder. Stir in beer to blend. 2. Add crawfish meat to batter and stir to coat. 3. Combine the coating ingredients in food processor and pulse to finely crush the crumbs. Transfer crumbs to shallow dish. 4. Preheat the zone 1 air fryer basket to 390°F (199°C). 5. Pour the crawfish and batter into a colander to drain. Stir with a spoon to drain excess batter. 6. Working with a handful of crawfish at a time, roll in crumbs and place on a cookie sheet. It's okay if some of the smaller pieces of crawfish meat stick together. 7. Spray breaded crawfish with oil or cooking spray and place all at once into the zone 1 air fryer basket. 8. Air fry at 390°F (199°C) for 5 minutes. Shake basket or stir and mist again with olive oil or spray. Cook 5 more minutes, shake basket again, and mist lightly again. Continue cooking 3 to 5 more minutes, until browned and crispy.
Make the Tandoori-Spiced Salmon (zone 2 basket): 1. Preheat the zone 2 air fryer basket to 375°F (191°C). 2. In a bowl, toss the potatoes with 1 tablespoon of the oil until evenly coated. Season with salt and pepper. Transfer the potatoes to the zone 2 air fryer basket and air fry for 20 minutes. 3. Meanwhile, in a bowl, combine the remaining 1 tablespoon oil, the turmeric, cumin, ginger, paprika, and cayenne. Add the salmon fillets and turn in the spice mixture until fully coated all over. 4. After the potatoes have cooked for 20 minutes, place the salmon fillets, skin-side up, on top of the potatoes, and continue cooking until the potatoes are tender, the salmon is cooked, and the salmon skin is slightly crisp. 5. Transfer the salmon fillets to two plates and serve with the potatoes while both are warm.

Fish Tacos with Jalapeño-Lime Sauce

Prep time: 25 minutes | Cook time: 7 to 10 minutes | Serves 4

Fish Tacos:
1 pound (454 g) fish fillets
¼ teaspoon cumin
¼ teaspoon coriander
⅛ teaspoon ground red pepper
1 tablespoon lime zest
¼ teaspoon smoked paprika
1 teaspoon oil
Cooking spray
6 to 8 corn or flour tortillas (6-inch size)
Jalapeño-Lime Sauce:
½ cup sour cream
1 tablespoon lime juice
¼ teaspoon grated lime zest
½ teaspoon minced jalapeño (flesh only)
¼ teaspoon cumin
Napa Cabbage Garnish:
1 cup shredded Napa cabbage
¼ cup slivered red or green bell pepper
¼ cup slivered onion

1. Slice the fish fillets into strips approximately ½-inch thick. 2. Put the strips into a sealable plastic bag along with the cumin, coriander, red pepper, lime zest, smoked paprika, and oil. Massage seasonings into the fish until evenly distributed. 3. Spray the two air fryer baskets with nonstick cooking spray and place seasoned fish inside. 4. Air fry at 390°F (199°C) for approximately 5 minutes. Shake baskets to distribute fish. Cook an additional 2 to 5 minutes, until fish flakes easily. 5. While the fish is cooking, prepare the Jalapeño-Lime Sauce by mixing the sour cream, lime juice, lime zest, jalapeño, and cumin together to make a smooth sauce. Set aside. 6. Mix the cabbage, bell pepper, and onion together and set aside. 7. To warm refrigerated tortillas, wrap in damp paper towels and microwave for 30 to 60 seconds. 8. To serve, spoon some of fish into a warm tortilla. Add one or two tablespoons Napa Cabbage Garnish and drizzle with Jalapeño-Lime Sauce.

Pecan-Crusted Tilapia

Prep time: 10 minutes | Cook time: 10 minutes | Serves 4

1¼ cups pecans
¾ cup panko bread crumbs
½ cup all-purpose flour
2 tablespoons Cajun seasoning

2 eggs, beaten with 2 tablespoons water
4 (6-ounce/ 170-g) tilapia fillets
Vegetable oil, for spraying
Lemon wedges, for serving

1. Grind the pecans in the food processor until they resemble coarse meal. Combine the ground pecans with the panko on a plate. On a second plate, combine the flour and Cajun seasoning. Dry the tilapia fillets using paper towels and dredge them in the flour mixture, shaking off any excess. Dip the fillets in the egg mixture and then dredge them in the pecan and panko mixture, pressing the coating onto the fillets. Place the breaded fillets on a plate or rack. 2. Preheat the air fryer to 375°F (191°C). Spray both sides of the breaded fillets with oil. Carefully transfer the fillets to the two air fryer baskets and air fry for 9 to 10 minutes, flipping once halfway through, until the flesh is opaque and flaky. 3. Serve immediately with lemon wedges.

Country Shrimp

Prep time: 10 minutes | Cook time: 15 to 20 minutes | Serves 4

1 pound (454 g) large shrimp, deveined, with tails on
1 pound (454 g) smoked turkey sausage, cut into thick slices
2 corn cobs, quartered
1 zucchini, cut into bite-sized pieces

1 red bell pepper, cut into chunks
1 tablespoon Old Bay seasoning
2 tablespoons olive oil
Cooking spray

1. Preheat the air fryer to 400°F (204°C). Spray the two air fryer baskets lightly with cooking spray. 2. In a large bowl, mix the shrimp, turkey sausage, corn, zucchini, bell pepper, and Old Bay seasoning, and toss to coat with the spices. Add the olive oil and toss again until evenly coated. 3. Spread the mixture in the two air fryer baskets in a single layer. 4. Air fry for 15 to 20 minutes, or until cooked through, shaking the baskets every 5 minutes for even cooking. 5. Serve immediately.

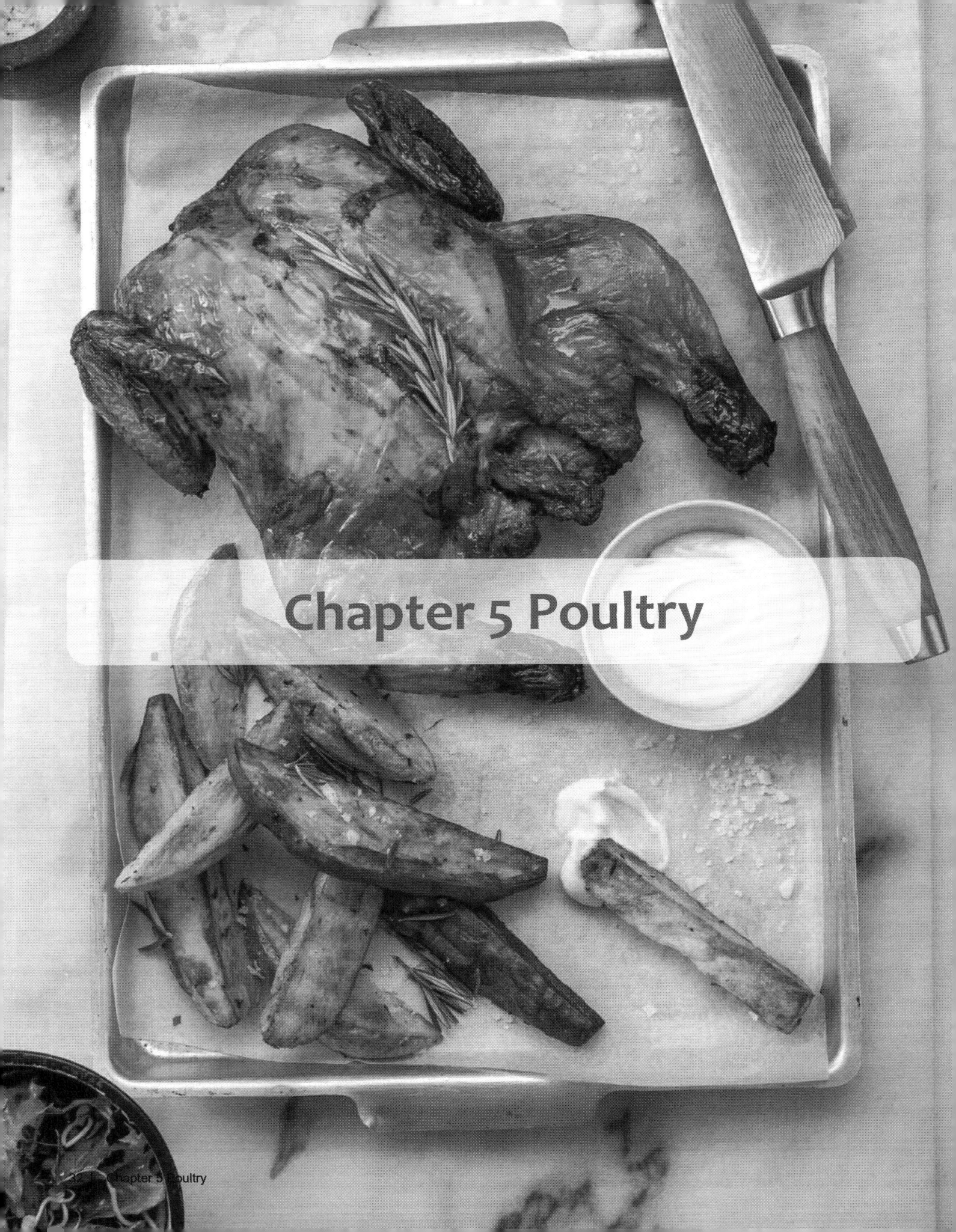

Chapter 5 Poultry

Chapter 5 Poultry

Butter and Bacon Chicken

Prep time: 10 minutes | Cook time: 65 minutes | Serves 6

1 (4-pound / 1.8-kg) whole chicken
2 tablespoons salted butter, softened
1 teaspoon dried thyme
½ teaspoon garlic powder
1 teaspoon salt
½ teaspoon ground black pepper
6 slices sugar-free bacon

1. Pat chicken dry with a paper towel, then rub with butter on all sides. Sprinkle thyme, garlic powder, salt, and pepper over chicken. 2. Place chicken into the ungreased zone 1 air fryer basket, breast side up. Lay strips of bacon over chicken and secure with toothpicks. 3. Adjust the temperature to 350°F (177°C) and air fry for 65 minutes. Halfway through cooking, remove and set aside bacon and flip chicken over. Chicken will be done when the skin is golden and crispy and the internal temperature is at least 165°F (74°C). Serve warm with bacon.

Porchetta-Style Chicken Breasts

Prep time: 10 minutes | Cook time: 15 minutes | Serves 4

½ cup fresh parsley leaves
¼ cup roughly chopped fresh chives
4 cloves garlic, peeled
2 tablespoons lemon juice
3 teaspoons fine sea salt
1 teaspoon dried rubbed sage
1 teaspoon fresh rosemary leaves
1 teaspoon ground fennel
½ teaspoon red pepper flakes
4 (4-ounce / 113-g) boneless, skinless chicken breasts, pounded to ¼ inch thick
8 slices bacon
Sprigs of fresh rosemary, for garnish (optional)

1. Spray the two air fryer baskets with avocado oil. Preheat the air fryer to 340°F (171°C). 2. Place the parsley, chives, garlic, lemon juice, salt, sage, rosemary, fennel, and red pepper flakes in a food processor and purée until a smooth paste forms. 3. Place the chicken breasts on a cutting board and rub the paste all over the tops. With a short end facing you, roll each breast up like a jelly roll to make a log and secure it with toothpicks. 4. Wrap 2 slices of bacon around each chicken breast log to cover the entire breast. Secure the bacon with toothpicks. 5. Place the chicken breast logs in the two air fryer baskets and air fry for 5 minutes, flip the logs over, and cook for another 5 minutes. Increase the heat to 390°F (199°C) and cook until the bacon is crisp, about 5 minutes more. 6. Remove the toothpicks and garnish with fresh rosemary sprigs, if desired, before serving. Store leftovers in an airtight container in the refrigerator for up to 4 days or in the freezer for up to a month. Reheat in a preheated 350°F (177°C) air fryer for 5 minutes, then increase the heat to 390°F (199°C) and cook for 2 minutes to crisp the bacon.

Chicken Schnitzel

Prep time: 15 minutes | Cook time: 5 minutes | Serves 4

½ cup all-purpose flour
1 teaspoon marjoram
½ teaspoon thyme
1 teaspoon dried parsley flakes
½ teaspoon salt
1 egg
1 teaspoon lemon juice
1 teaspoon water
1 cup breadcrumbs
4 chicken tenders, pounded thin, cut in half lengthwise
Cooking spray

1. Preheat the air fryer to 390°F (199°C) and spritz with cooking spray. 2. Combine the flour, marjoram, thyme, parsley, and salt in a shallow dish. Stir to mix well. 3. Whisk the egg with lemon juice and water in a large bowl. Pour the breadcrumbs in a separate shallow dish. 4. Roll the chicken halves in the flour mixture first, then in the egg mixture, and then roll over the breadcrumbs to coat well. Shake the excess off. 5. Arrange the chicken halves in the preheated air fryer and spritz with cooking spray on both sides. 6. Air fry for 5 minutes or until the chicken halves are golden brown and crispy. Flip the halves halfway through. 7. Serve immediately.

Bacon-Wrapped Chicken Breasts Rolls

Prep time: 10 minutes | Cook time: 15 minutes | Serves 4

¼ cup chopped fresh chives
2 tablespoons lemon juice
1 teaspoon dried sage
1 teaspoon fresh rosemary leaves
½ cup fresh parsley leaves
4 cloves garlic, peeled
1 teaspoon ground fennel
3 teaspoons sea salt
½ teaspoon red pepper flakes
4 (4-ounce / 113-g) boneless, skinless chicken breasts, pounded to ¼ inch thick
8 slices bacon
Sprigs of fresh rosemary, for garnish
Cooking spray

1. Preheat the air fryer to 340°F (171°C). Spritz the two air fryer baskets with cooking spray. 2. Put the chives, lemon juice, sage, rosemary, parsley, garlic, fennel, salt, and red pepper flakes in a food processor, then pulse to purée until smooth. 3. Unfold the chicken breasts on a clean work surface, then brush the top side of the chicken breasts with the sauce. 4. Roll the chicken breasts up from the shorter side, then wrap each chicken rolls with 2 bacon slices to cover. Secure with toothpicks. 5. Arrange the rolls in the preheated air fryer baskets, then cook for 10 minutes. Flip the rolls halfway through. 6. Increase the heat to 390°F (199°C) and air fry for 5 more minutes or until the bacon is browned and crispy. 7. Transfer the rolls to a large plate. Discard the toothpicks and spread with rosemary sprigs before serving.

Gold Livers

Prep time: 10 minutes | Cook time: 20 minutes | Serves 4

- 2 eggs
- 2 tablespoons water
- ¾ cup flour
- 2 cups panko breadcrumbs
- 1 teaspoon salt
- ½ teaspoon ground black pepper
- 20 ounces (567 g) chicken livers
- Cooking spray

1. Preheat the air fryer to 390°F (199°C). Spritz the two air fryer baskets with cooking spray. 2. Whisk the eggs with water in a large bowl. Pour the flour in a separate bowl. Pour the panko on a shallow dish and sprinkle with salt and pepper. 3. Dredge the chicken livers in the flour. Shake the excess off, then dunk the livers in the whisked eggs, and then roll the livers over the panko to coat well. 4. Arrange the livers in the preheated two air fryer baskets and spritz with cooking spray. 5. Air fry for 10 minutes or until the livers are golden and crispy. Flip the livers halfway through. 6. Serve immediately.

Honey-Glazed Chicken Thighs and Peachy Chicken Chunks with Cherries

Prep time: 13 minutes | Cook time: 16 minutes | Serves 8

- Honey-Glazed Chicken Thighs:
- Oil, for spraying
- 4 boneless, skinless chicken thighs, fat trimmed
- 3 tablespoons soy sauce
- 1 tablespoon balsamic vinegar
- 2 teaspoons honey
- 2 teaspoons minced garlic
- 1 teaspoon ground ginger
- Peachy Chicken Chunks with Cherries:
- ⅓ cup peach preserves
- 1 teaspoon ground rosemary
- ½ teaspoon black pepper
- ½ teaspoon salt
- ½ teaspoon marjoram
- 1 teaspoon light olive oil
- 1 pound (454 g) boneless chicken breasts, cut in 1½-inch chunks
- Oil for misting or cooking spray
- 1 (10-ounce / 283-g) package frozen unsweetened dark cherries, thawed and drained

Make the Honey-Glazed Chicken Thighs (zone 1 basket): 1. Preheat the zone 1 air fryer basket to 400°F (204°C). Line the zone 1 air fryer basket with parchment and spray lightly with oil. 2. Place the chicken in the prepared basket. 3. Cook for 7 minutes, flip, and cook for another 7 minutes, or until the internal temperature reaches 165°F (74°C) and the juices run clear. 4. In a small saucepan, combine the soy sauce, balsamic vinegar, honey, garlic, and ginger and cook over low heat for 1 to 2 minutes, until warmed through. 5. Transfer the chicken to a serving plate and drizzle with the sauce just before serving.
Make the Peachy Chicken Chunks with Cherries (zone 2 basket): 1. In a medium bowl, mix together peach preserves, rosemary, pepper, salt, marjoram, and olive oil. 2. Stir in chicken chunks and toss to coat well with the preserve mixture. 3. Spray the zone 2 air fryer basket with oil or cooking spray and lay chicken chunks in basket. 4. Air fry at 390°F (199°C) for 7 minutes. Stir. Cook for 6 to 8 more minutes or until chicken juices run clear. 5. When chicken has cooked through, scatter the cherries over and cook for additional minute to heat cherries.

Apricot Chicken and Jerk Chicken Kebabs

Prep time: 25 minutes | Cook time: 14 minutes | Serves 8

- Apricot Chicken:
- ⅔ cup apricot preserves
- 2 tablespoons freshly squeezed lemon juice
- 1 teaspoon soy sauce
- ¼ teaspoon salt
- ¾ cup panko bread crumbs
- 2 whole boneless, skinless chicken breasts (1 pound / 454 g each), halved
- 1 to 2 tablespoons oil
- Jerk Chicken Kebabs:
- 8 ounces (227 g) boneless, skinless chicken thighs, cut into 1-inch cubes
- 2 tablespoons jerk seasoning
- 2 tablespoons coconut oil
- ½ medium red bell pepper, seeded and cut into 1-inch pieces
- ¼ medium red onion, peeled and cut into 1-inch pieces
- ½ teaspoon salt

Make the Apricot Chicken (zone 1 basket): 1. In a shallow bowl, stir together the apricot preserves, lemon juice, soy sauce, and salt. Place the bread crumbs in a second shallow bowl. 2. Roll the chicken in the preserves mixture and then the bread crumbs, coating thoroughly. 3. Preheat the zone 1 air fryer basket to 350°F (177°C). Line the zone 1 air fryer basket with parchment paper. 4. Place the coated chicken on the parchment and spritz with oil. 5. Cook for 5 minutes. Flip the chicken, spritz it with oil, and cook for 5 to 7 minutes more until the internal temperature reaches 165°F (74°C) and the chicken is no longer pink inside. Let sit for 5 minutes.
Make the Jerk Chicken Kebabs (zone 2 basket): 1. Place chicken in a medium bowl and sprinkle with jerk seasoning and coconut oil. Toss to coat on all sides. 2. Using eight (6-inch) skewers, build skewers by alternating chicken, pepper, and onion pieces, about three repetitions per skewer. 3. Sprinkle salt over skewers and place into ungreased zone 2 air fryer basket. Adjust the temperature to 370°F (188°C) and air fry for 14 minutes, turning skewers halfway through cooking. Chicken will be golden and have an internal temperature of at least 165°F (74°C) when done. Serve warm.

Hoisin Turkey Burgers

Prep time: 30 minutes | Cook time: 20 minutes | Serves 4

- Olive oil
- 1 pound (454 g) lean ground turkey
- ¼ cup whole-wheat bread crumbs
- ¼ cup hoisin sauce
- 2 tablespoons soy sauce
- 4 whole-wheat buns

1. Spray the two air fryer baskets lightly with olive oil. 2. In a large bowl, mix together the turkey, bread crumbs, hoisin sauce, and soy sauce. 3. Form the mixture into 4 equal patties. Cover with plastic wrap and refrigerate the patties for 30 minutes. 4. Place the patties in the two air fryer baskets in a single layer. Spray the patties lightly with olive oil. 5. Air fry at 370°F (188°C) for 10 minutes. Flip the patties over, lightly spray with olive oil, and cook until golden brown, an additional 5 to 10 minutes. 6. Place the patties on buns and top with your choice of low-calorie burger toppings like sliced tomatoes, onions, and cabbage slaw.

Lemon Chicken

Prep time: 5 minutes | Cook time: 20 to 25 minutes | Serves 4

8 bone-in chicken thighs, skin on	½ teaspoon paprika
1 tablespoon olive oil	½ teaspoon garlic powder
1½ teaspoons lemon-pepper seasoning	¼ teaspoon freshly ground black pepper
	Juice of ½ lemon

1. Preheat the air fryer to 360ºF (182ºC). 2. Place the chicken in a large bowl and drizzle with the olive oil. Top with the lemon-pepper seasoning, paprika, garlic powder, and freshly ground black pepper. Toss until thoroughly coated. 3. Arrange the chicken in a single layer in the two baskets of the air fryer. Pausing halfway through the cooking time to turn the chicken, air fry for 20 to 25 minutes, until a thermometer inserted into the thickest piece registers 165ºF (74ºC). 4. Transfer the chicken to a serving platter and squeeze the lemon juice over the top.

Spice-Rubbed Chicken Thighs and Herb-Buttermilk Chicken Breast

Prep time: 15 minutes | Cook time: 40 minutes | Serves 6

Spice-Rubbed Chicken Thighs:	1 large bone-in, skin-on chicken breast
4 (4-ounce / 113-g) bone-in, skin-on chicken thighs	1 cup buttermilk
½ teaspoon salt	1½ teaspoons dried parsley
½ teaspoon garlic powder	1½ teaspoons dried chives
2 teaspoons chili powder	¾ teaspoon kosher salt
1 teaspoon paprika	½ teaspoon dried dill
1 teaspoon ground cumin	½ teaspoon onion powder
1 small lime, halved	¼ teaspoon garlic powder
Herb-Buttermilk Chicken Breast:	¼ teaspoon dried tarragon
	Cooking spray

Spice-Rubbed Chicken Thighs (zone 1 basket): 1. Pat chicken thighs dry and sprinkle with salt, garlic powder, chili powder, paprika, and cumin. 2. Squeeze juice from ½ lime over thighs. Place thighs into the ungreased zone 1 air fryer basket. Adjust the temperature to 380ºF (193ºC) and roast for 25 minutes, turning thighs halfway through cooking. Thighs will be crispy and browned with an internal temperature of at least 165ºF (74ºC) when done. 3. Transfer thighs to a large serving plate and drizzle with remaining lime juice. Serve warm.
Herb-Buttermilk Chicken Breast (zone 2 basket): 1. Place the chicken breast in a bowl and pour over the buttermilk, turning the chicken in it to make sure it's completely covered. Let the chicken stand at room temperature for at least 20 minutes or in the refrigerator for up to 4 hours. 2. Meanwhile, in a bowl, stir together the parsley, chives, salt, dill, onion powder, garlic powder, and tarragon. 3. Preheat the zone 2 air fryer basket to 300ºF (149ºC). 4. Remove the chicken from the buttermilk, letting the excess drip off, then place the chicken skin-side up directly in the zone 2 air fryer basket. Sprinkle the seasoning mix all over the top of the chicken breast, then let stand until the herb mix soaks into the buttermilk, at least 5 minutes. 5. Spray the top of the chicken with cooking spray. Bake for 10 minutes, then increase the temperature to 350ºF (177ºC) and bake until an instant-read thermometer inserted into the thickest part of the breast reads 160ºF (71ºC) and the chicken is deep golden brown, 30 to 35 minutes. 6. Transfer the chicken breast to a cutting board, let rest for 10 minutes, then cut the meat off the bone and cut into thick slices for serving.

Spice-Rubbed Turkey Breast

Prep time: 5 minutes | Cook time: 45 to 55 minutes | Serves 10

1 tablespoon sea salt	pepper
1 teaspoon paprika	4 pounds (1.8 kg) bone-in, skin-on turkey breast
1 teaspoon onion powder	2 tablespoons unsalted butter, melted
1 teaspoon garlic powder	
½ teaspoon freshly ground black	

1. In a small bowl, combine the salt, paprika, onion powder, garlic powder, and pepper. 2. Sprinkle the seasonings all over the turkey. Brush the turkey with some of the melted butter. 3. Set the air fryer to 350ºF (177ºC). Place the turkey in the two air fryer baskets, skin-side down, and roast for 25 minutes. 4. Flip the turkey and brush it with the remaining butter. Continue cooking for another 20 to 30 minutes, until an instant-read thermometer reads 160ºF (71ºC). 5. Remove the turkey breast from the air fryer. Tent a piece of aluminum foil over the turkey, and allow it to rest for about 5 minutes before serving.

Cracked-Pepper Chicken Wings and Buffalo Chicken Cheese Sticks

Prep time: 20 minutes | Cook time: 20 minutes | Serves 6

Cracked-Pepper Chicken Wings:	black pepper
1 pound (454 g) chicken wings	Buffalo Chicken Cheese Sticks:
3 tablespoons vegetable oil	1 cup shredded cooked chicken
½ cup all-purpose flour	¼ cup buffalo sauce
½ teaspoon smoked paprika	1 cup shredded Mozzarella cheese
½ teaspoon garlic powder	1 large egg
½ teaspoon kosher salt	¼ cup crumbled feta
1½ teaspoons freshly cracked	

Make the Cracked-Pepper Chicken Wings (zone 1 basket): 1. Place the chicken wings in a large bowl. Drizzle the vegetable oil over wings and toss to coat. 2. In a separate bowl, whisk together the flour, paprika, garlic powder, salt, and pepper until combined. 3. Dredge the wings in the flour mixture one at a time, coating them well, and place in the zone 1 air fryer basket. Set the temperature to 400ºF (204ºC) for 20 minutes, turning the wings halfway through the cooking time, until the breading is browned and crunchy.
Make the Buffalo Chicken Cheese Sticks (zone 2 basket): 1. In a large bowl, mix all ingredients except the feta. Cut a piece of parchment to fit your air fryer basket and press the mixture into a ½-inch-thick circle. 2. Sprinkle the mixture with feta and place into the zone 2 air fryer basket. 3. Adjust the temperature to 400ºF (204ºC) and air fry for 8 minutes. 4. After 5 minutes, flip over the cheese mixture. 5. Allow to cool 5 minutes before cutting into sticks. Serve warm.

Yakitori

Prep time: 10 minutes | Cook time: 15 minutes | Serves 4

½ cup mirin
¼ cup dry white wine
½ cup soy sauce
1 tablespoon light brown sugar
1½ pounds (680 g) boneless, skinless chicken thighs, cut into 1½-inch pieces, fat trimmed
4 medium scallions, trimmed, cut into 1½-inch pieces
Cooking spray
Special Equipment:
4 (4-inch) bamboo skewers, soaked in water for at least 30 minutes

1. Combine the mirin, dry white wine, soy sauce, and brown sugar in a saucepan. Bring to a boil over medium heat. Keep stirring. 2. Boil for another 2 minutes or until it has a thick consistency. Turn off the heat. 3. Preheat the air fryer to 400°F (204°C). Spritz the two air fryer baskets with cooking spray. 4. Run the bamboo skewers through the chicken pieces and scallions alternatively. 5. Arrange the skewers in the preheated air fryer, then brush with mirin mixture on both sides. Spritz with cooking spray. 6. Air fry for 10 minutes or until the chicken and scallions are glossy. Flip the skewers halfway through. 7. Serve immediately.

Easy Turkey Tenderloin

Prep time: 20 minutes | Cook time: 30 minutes | Serves 4

Olive oil
½ teaspoon paprika
½ teaspoon garlic powder
½ teaspoon salt
½ teaspoon freshly ground black pepper
Pinch cayenne pepper
1½ pounds (680 g) turkey breast tenderloin

1. Spray the two air fryer baskets lightly with olive oil. 2. In a small bowl, combine the paprika, garlic powder, salt, black pepper, and cayenne pepper. Rub the mixture all over the turkey. 3. Place the turkey in the air fryer baskets and lightly spray with olive oil. 4. Air fry at 370°F (188°C) for 15 minutes. Flip the turkey over and lightly spray with olive oil. Air fry until the internal temperature reaches at least 170°F (77°C) for an additional 10 to 15 minutes. 5. Let the turkey rest for 10 minutes before slicing and serving.

Jerk Chicken Thighs

Prep time: 30 minutes | Cook time: 15 to 20 minutes | Serves 6

2 teaspoons ground coriander
1 teaspoon ground allspice
1 teaspoon cayenne pepper
1 teaspoon ground ginger
1 teaspoon salt
1 teaspoon dried thyme
½ teaspoon ground cinnamon
½ teaspoon ground nutmeg
2 pounds (907 g) boneless chicken thighs, skin on
2 tablespoons olive oil

1. In a small bowl, combine the coriander, allspice, cayenne, ginger, salt, thyme, cinnamon, and nutmeg. Stir until thoroughly combined. 2. Place the chicken in a baking dish and use paper towels to pat dry. Thoroughly coat both sides of the chicken with the spice mixture. Cover and refrigerate for at least 2 hours, preferably overnight. 3. Preheat the air fryer to 360°F (182°C). 4. Arrange the chicken in a single layer in the two air fryer baskets and lightly coat with the olive oil. Pausing halfway through the cooking time to flip the chicken, air fry for 15 to 20 minutes, until a thermometer inserted into the thickest part registers 165°F (74°C).

Brazilian Tempero Baiano Chicken Drumsticks

Prep time: 30 minutes | Cook time: 20 minutes | Serves 4

1 teaspoon cumin seeds
1 teaspoon dried oregano
1 teaspoon dried parsley
1 teaspoon ground turmeric
½ teaspoon coriander seeds
1 teaspoon kosher salt
½ teaspoon black peppercorns
½ teaspoon cayenne pepper
¼ cup fresh lime juice
2 tablespoons olive oil
1½ pounds (680 g) chicken drumsticks

1. In a clean coffee grinder or spice mill, combine the cumin, oregano, parsley, turmeric, coriander seeds, salt, peppercorns, and cayenne. Process until finely ground. 2. In a small bowl, combine the ground spices with the lime juice and oil. Place the chicken in a resealable plastic bag. Add the marinade, seal, and massage until the chicken is well coated. Marinate at room temperature for 30 minutes or in the refrigerator for up to 24 hours. 3. When you are ready to cook, place the drumsticks skin side up in the two air fryer baskets. Set the air fryer to 400°F (204°C) for 20 to 25 minutes, turning the legs halfway through the cooking time. Use a meat thermometer to ensure that the chicken has reached an internal temperature of 165°F (74°C). 4. Serve with plenty of napkins.

Tandoori Chicken

Prep time: 30 minutes | Cook time: 15 minutes | Serves 4

1 pound (454 g) chicken tenders, halved crosswise
¼ cup plain Greek yogurt
1 tablespoon minced fresh ginger
1 tablespoon minced garlic
¼ cup chopped fresh cilantro or parsley
1 teaspoon kosher salt
½ to 1 teaspoon cayenne pepper
1 teaspoon ground turmeric
1 teaspoon garam masala
1 teaspoon sweet smoked paprika
1 tablespoon vegetable oil or melted ghee
2 teaspoons fresh lemon juice
2 tablespoons chopped fresh cilantro

1. In a large glass bowl, toss together the chicken, yogurt, ginger, garlic, cilantro, salt, cayenne, turmeric, garam masala, and paprika to coat. Marinate at room temperature for 30 minutes, or cover and refrigerate for up to 24 hours. 2. Place the chicken in a single layer in the two air fryer baskets. (Discard remaining marinade.) Spray the chicken with oil. Set the air fryer to 350°F (177°C) for 15 minutes. Halfway through the cooking time, spray the chicken with more vegetable oil spray, and toss gently to coat. Cook for 5 minutes more. 3. Transfer the chicken to a serving platter. Sprinkle with lemon juice and toss to coat. Sprinkle with the cilantro and serve.

Broccoli Cheese Chicken

Prep time: 10 minutes | Cook time: 19 to 24 minutes | Serves 6

1 tablespoon avocado oil
¼ cup chopped onion
½ cup finely chopped broccoli
4 ounces (113 g) cream cheese, at room temperature
2 ounces (57 g) Cheddar cheese, shredded
1 teaspoon garlic powder
½ teaspoon sea salt, plus additional for seasoning, divided
¼ freshly ground black pepper, plus additional for seasoning, divided
2 pounds (907 g) boneless, skinless chicken breasts
1 teaspoon smoked paprika

1. Heat a medium skillet over medium-high heat and pour in the avocado oil. Add the onion and broccoli and cook, stirring occasionally, for 5 to 8 minutes, until the onion is tender. 2. Transfer to a large bowl and stir in the cream cheese, Cheddar cheese, and garlic powder, and season to taste with salt and pepper. 3. Hold a sharp knife parallel to the chicken breast and cut a long pocket into one side. Stuff the chicken pockets with the broccoli mixture, using toothpicks to secure the pockets around the filling. 4. In a small dish, combine the paprika, ½ teaspoon salt, and ¼ teaspoon pepper. Sprinkle this over the outside of the chicken. 5. Set the air fryer to 400°F (204°C). Place the chicken in a single layer in the two air fryer baskets, and cook for 14 to 16 minutes, until an instant-read thermometer reads 160°F (71°C). Place the chicken on a plate and tent a piece of aluminum foil over the chicken. Allow to rest for 5 to 10 minutes before serving.

Teriyaki Chicken Legs and Bell Pepper Stuffed Chicken Roll-Ups

Prep time: 22 minutes | Cook time: 18 to 20 minutes | Serves 6

Teriyaki Chicken Legs:
4 tablespoons teriyaki sauce
1 tablespoon orange juice
1 teaspoon smoked paprika
4 chicken legs
Cooking spray
Bell Pepper Stuffed Chicken Roll-Ups:
2 (4-ounce / 113-g) boneless, skinless chicken breasts, slice in half horizontally
1 tablespoon olive oil
Juice of ½ lime
2 tablespoons taco seasoning
½ green bell pepper, cut into strips
½ red bell pepper, cut into strips
¼ onion, sliced

Make the Teriyaki Chicken Legs (zone 1 basket): 1. Mix together the teriyaki sauce, orange juice, and smoked paprika. Brush on all sides of chicken legs. 2. Spray the zone 1 air fryer basket with nonstick cooking spray and place chicken in basket. 3. Air fry at 360°F (182°C) for 6 minutes. Turn and baste with sauce. Cook for 6 more minutes, turn and baste. Cook for 6 to 8 minutes more, until juices run clear when chicken is pierced with a fork.
Make the Bell Pepper Stuffed Chicken Roll-Ups (zone 2 basket): 1. Preheat the zone 2 air fryer basket to 400°F (204°C). 2. Unfold the chicken breast slices on a clean work surface. Rub with olive oil, then drizzle with lime juice and sprinkle with taco seasoning. 3. Top the chicken slices with equal amount of bell peppers and onion. Roll them up and secure with toothpicks. 4. Arrange the chicken roll-ups in the preheated air fryer basket. Air fry for 12 minutes or until the internal temperature of the chicken reaches at least 165°F (74°C). Flip the chicken roll-ups halfway through. 5. Remove the chicken from the air fryer. Discard the toothpicks and serve immediately.

Sweet and Spicy Turkey Meatballs

Prep time: 15 minutes | Cook time: 15 minutes | Serves 6

Olive oil
1 pound (454 g) lean ground turkey
½ cup whole-wheat panko bread crumbs
1 egg, beaten
1 tablespoon soy sauce
¼ cup plus 1 tablespoon hoisin sauce, divided
2 teaspoons minced garlic
⅛ teaspoon salt
⅛ teaspoon freshly ground black pepper
1 teaspoon Sriracha

1. Spray the two air fryer baskets lightly with olive oil. 2. In a large bowl, mix together the turkey, panko bread crumbs, egg, soy sauce, 1 tablespoon of hoisin sauce, garlic, salt, and black pepper. 3. Using a tablespoon, form 24 meatballs. 4. In a small bowl, combine the remaining ¼ cup of hoisin sauce and Sriracha to make a glaze and set aside. 5. Place the meatballs in the two air fryer baskets in a single layer. 6. Air fry at 350°F (177°C) for 8 minutes. Brush the meatballs generously with the glaze and cook until cooked through, an additional 4 to 7 minutes.

South Indian Pepper Chicken

Prep time: 30 minutes | Cook time: 15 minutes | Serves 4

Spice Mix:
1 dried red chile, or ½ teaspoon dried red pepper flakes
1-inch piece cinnamon or cassia bark
1½ teaspoons coriander seeds
1 teaspoon fennel seeds
1 teaspoon cumin seeds
1 teaspoon black peppercorns
½ teaspoon cardamom seeds
¼ teaspoon ground turmeric
1 teaspoon kosher salt
Chicken:
1 pound (454 g) boneless, skinless chicken thighs, cut crosswise into thirds
2 medium onions, cut into ½-inch-thick slices
¼ cup olive oil
Cauliflower rice, steamed rice, or naan bread, for serving

1. For the spice mix: Combine the dried chile, cinnamon, coriander, fennel, cumin, peppercorns, and cardamom in a clean coffee or spice grinder. Grind, shaking the grinder lightly so all the seeds and bits get into the blades, until the mixture is broken down to a fine powder. Stir in the turmeric and salt. 2. For the chicken: Place the chicken and onions in resealable plastic bag. Add the oil and 1½ tablespoons of the spice mix. Seal the bag and massage until the chicken is well coated. Marinate at room temperature for 30 minutes or in the refrigerator for up to 24 hours. 3. Place the chicken and onions in the two air fryer baskets. Set the air fryer to 350°F (177°C) for 10 minutes, stirring once halfway through the cooking time. Increase the temperature to 400°F (204°C) for 5 minutes. Use a meat thermometer to ensure the chicken has reached an internal temperature of 165°F (74°C). 4. Serve with steamed rice, cauliflower rice, or naan.

Nashville Hot Chicken

Prep time: 20 minutes | Cook time: 24 to 28 minutes | Serves 8

3 pounds (1.4 kg) bone-in, skin-on chicken pieces, breasts halved crosswise
1 tablespoon sea salt
1 tablespoon freshly ground black pepper
1½ cups finely ground blanched almond flour
1½ cups grated Parmesan cheese
1 tablespoon baking powder
2 teaspoons garlic powder, divided
½ cup heavy (whipping) cream
2 large eggs, beaten
1 tablespoon vinegar-based hot sauce
Avocado oil spray
½ cup (1 stick) unsalted butter
½ cup avocado oil
1 tablespoon cayenne pepper (more or less to taste)
2 tablespoons Swerve

1. Sprinkle the chicken with the salt and pepper. 2. In a large shallow bowl, whisk together the almond flour, Parmesan cheese, baking powder, and 1 teaspoon of the garlic powder. 3. In a separate bowl, whisk together the heavy cream, eggs, and hot sauce. 4. Dip the chicken pieces in the egg, then coat each with the almond flour mixture, pressing the mixture into the chicken to adhere. Allow to sit for 15 minutes to let the breading set. 5. Set the air fryer to 400°F (204°C). Place the chicken in a single layer in the two air fryer baskets, being careful not to overcrowd the pieces. Spray the chicken with oil and roast for 13 minutes. 6. Carefully flip the chicken and spray it with more oil. Reduce the air fryer temperature to 350°F (177°C). Roast for another 11 to 15 minutes, until an instant-read thermometer reads 160°F (71°C). 7. While the chicken cooks, heat the butter, avocado oil, cayenne pepper, Swerve, and remaining 1 teaspoon of garlic powder in a saucepan over medium-low heat. Cook until the butter is melted and the sugar substitute has dissolved. 8. Remove the chicken from the air fryer. Use tongs to dip the chicken in the sauce. Place the coated chicken on a rack over a baking sheet, and allow it to rest for 5 minutes before serving.

Stuffed Chicken Florentine

Prep time: 10 minutes | Cook time: 20 minutes | Serves 4

3 tablespoons pine nuts
¾ cup frozen spinach, thawed and squeezed dry
⅓ cup ricotta cheese
2 tablespoons grated Parmesan cheese
3 cloves garlic, minced
Salt and freshly ground black pepper, to taste
4 small boneless, skinless chicken breast halves (about 1½ pounds / 680 g)
8 slices bacon

1. Place the pine nuts in two small pans and separately set in the two air fryer baskets. Set the air fryer to 400°F (204°C) and air fry for 2 to 3 minutes until toasted. Remove the pine nuts to a mixing bowl and continue preheating the air fryer. 2. In a large bowl, combine the spinach, ricotta, Parmesan, and garlic. Season to taste with salt and pepper and stir well until thoroughly combined. 3. Using a sharp knife, cut into the chicken breasts, slicing them across and opening them up like a book, but be careful not to cut them all the way through. Sprinkle the chicken with salt and pepper. 4. Spoon equal amounts of the spinach mixture into the chicken, then fold the top of the chicken breast back over the top of the stuffing. Wrap each chicken breast with 2 slices of bacon. 5. Air fry the chicken for 18 to 20 minutes until the bacon is crisp and a thermometer inserted into the thickest part of the chicken registers 165°F (74°C).

Blackened Cajun Chicken Tenders

Prep time: 10 minutes | Cook time: 17 minutes | Serves 4

2 teaspoons paprika
1 teaspoon chili powder
½ teaspoon garlic powder
½ teaspoon dried thyme
¼ teaspoon onion powder
⅛ teaspoon ground cayenne pepper
2 tablespoons coconut oil
1 pound (454 g) boneless, skinless chicken tenders
¼ cup full-fat ranch dressing

1. In a small bowl, combine all seasonings. 2. Drizzle oil over chicken tenders and then generously coat each tender in the spice mixture. Place tenders into the two air fryer baskets. 3. Adjust the temperature to 375°F (191°C) and air fry for 17 minutes. 4. Tenders will be 165°F (74°C) internally when fully cooked. Serve with ranch dressing for dipping.

Cobb Salad

Prep time: 15 minutes | Cook time: 8 minutes | Serves 4-6

8 slices reduced-sodium bacon
8 chicken breast tenders (about 1½ pounds / 680 g)
8 cups chopped romaine lettuce
1 cup cherry tomatoes, halved
¼ red onion, thinly sliced
2 hard-boiled eggs, peeled and sliced
Avocado-Lime Dressing:
½ cup plain Greek yogurt
¼ cup almond milk
½ avocado
Juice of ½ lime
3 scallions, coarsely chopped
1 clove garlic
2 tablespoons fresh cilantro
⅛ teaspoon ground cumin
Salt and freshly ground black pepper, to taste

1. Preheat the air fryer to 400°F (204°C). 2. Wrap a piece of bacon around each piece of chicken and secure with a toothpick. Arrange the bacon-wrapped chicken in a single layer in the two air fryer baskets. Air fry for 8 minutes until the bacon is browned and a thermometer inserted into the thickest piece of chicken register 165°F (74°C). Let cool for a few minutes, then slice into bite-size pieces. 3. To make the dressing: In a blender or food processor, combine the yogurt, milk, avocado, lime juice, scallions, garlic, cilantro, and cumin. Purée until smooth. Season to taste with salt and freshly ground pepper. 4. To assemble the salad, in a large bowl, combine the lettuce, tomatoes, and onion. Drizzle the dressing over the vegetables and toss gently until thoroughly combined. Arrange the chicken and eggs on top just before serving.

Chicken Wings with Piri Piri Sauce

Prep time: 30 minutes | Cook time: 30 minutes | Serves 6

12 chicken wings
1½ ounces (43 g) butter, melted
1 teaspoon onion powder
½ teaspoon cumin powder
1 teaspoon garlic paste
Sauce:
2 ounces (57 g) piri piri peppers, stemmed and chopped
1 tablespoon pimiento, seeded and minced
1 garlic clove, chopped
2 tablespoons fresh lemon juice
⅓ teaspoon sea salt
½ teaspoon tarragon

1. Steam the chicken wings using a steamer basket that is placed over a saucepan with boiling water; reduce the heat. 2. Now, steam the wings for 10 minutes over a moderate heat. Toss the wings with butter, onion powder, cumin powder, and garlic paste. 3. Let the chicken wings cool to room temperature. Then, refrigerate them for 45 to 50 minutes. 4. Roast in the two preheated air fryer baskets at 330°F (166°C) for 25 to 30 minutes; make sure to flip them halfway through. 5. While the chicken wings are cooking, prepare the sauce by mixing all of the sauce ingredients in a food processor. Toss the wings with prepared Piri Piri Sauce and serve.

Buttermilk-Fried Drumsticks and Garlic Soy Chicken Thighs

Prep time: 20 minutes | Cook time: 30 minutes | Serves 3-4

Buttermilk-Fried Drumsticks:
1 egg
½ cup buttermilk
¾ cup self-rising flour
¾ cup seasoned panko bread crumbs
1 teaspoon salt
¼ teaspoon ground black pepper (to mix into coating)
4 chicken drumsticks, skin on
Oil for misting or cooking spray
Garlic Soy Chicken Thighs:
2 tablespoons chicken stock
2 tablespoons reduced-sodium soy sauce
1½ tablespoons sugar
4 garlic cloves, smashed and peeled
2 large scallions, cut into 2- to 3-inch batons, plus more, thinly sliced, for garnish
2 bone-in, skin-on chicken thighs (7 to 8 ounces / 198 to 227 g each)

Make the Buttermilk-Fried Drumsticks (zone 1 basket): 1. Beat together egg and buttermilk in shallow dish. 2. In a second shallow dish, combine the flour, panko crumbs, salt, and pepper. 3. Sprinkle chicken legs with additional salt and pepper to taste. 4. Dip legs in buttermilk mixture, then roll in panko mixture, pressing in crumbs to make coating stick. Mist with oil or cooking spray. 5. Spray the zone 1 air fryer basket with cooking spray. 6. Cook drumsticks at 360°F (182°C) for 10 minutes. Turn pieces over and cook an additional 10 minutes. 7. Turn pieces to check for browning. If you have any white spots that haven't begun to brown, spritz them with oil or cooking spray. Continue cooking for 5 more minutes or until crust is golden brown and juices run clear. Larger, meatier drumsticks will take longer to cook than small ones.
Make the Garlic Soy Chicken Thighs: 1. Preheat the zone 2 air fryer basket to 375°F (191°C). 2. In a metal cake pan, combine the chicken stock, soy sauce, and sugar and stir until the sugar dissolves. Add the garlic cloves, scallions, and chicken thighs, turning the thighs to coat them in the marinade, then resting them skin-side up. Place the pan in the zone 2 air fryer basket and bake, flipping the thighs every 5 minutes after the first 10 minutes, until the chicken is cooked through and the marinade is reduced to a sticky glaze over the chicken, about 30 minutes. 3. Remove the pan from the air fryer and serve the chicken thighs warm, with any remaining glaze spooned over top and sprinkled with more sliced scallions.

Wild Rice and Kale Stuffed Chicken Thighs

Prep time: 10 minutes | Cook time: 22 minutes | Serves 4

4 boneless, skinless chicken thighs
1 cup cooked wild rice
½ cup chopped kale
2 garlic cloves, minced
1 teaspoon salt
Juice of 1 lemon
½ cup crumbled feta
Olive oil cooking spray
1 tablespoon olive oil

1. Preheat the air fryer to 380°F (193°C). 2. Place the chicken thighs between two pieces of plastic wrap, and using a meat mallet or a rolling pin, pound them out to about ¼-inch thick. 3. In a medium bowl, combine the rice, kale, garlic, salt, and lemon juice and mix well. 4. Place a quarter of the rice mixture into the middle of each chicken thigh, then sprinkle 2 tablespoons of feta over the filling. 5. Spray the two air fryer baskets with olive oil cooking spray. 6. Fold the sides of the chicken thigh over the filling, and then gently place each of them seam-side down into the air fryer baskets. Brush each stuffed chicken thigh with olive oil. 7. Roast the stuffed chicken thighs for 12 minutes, then turn them over and cook for an additional 10 minutes, or until the internal temperature reaches 165°F (74°C).

Buffalo Chicken Wings

Prep time: 10 minutes | Cook time: 20 to 25 minutes | Serves 4

2 tablespoons baking powder
1 teaspoon smoked paprika
Sea salt and freshly ground black pepper, to taste
2 pounds (907 g) chicken wings or chicken drumettes
Avocado oil spray
⅓ cup avocado oil
½ cup Buffalo hot sauce, such as Frank's RedHot
¼ cup (4 tablespoons) unsalted butter
2 tablespoons apple cider vinegar
1 teaspoon minced garlic

1. In a large bowl, stir together the baking powder, smoked paprika, and salt and pepper to taste. Add the chicken wings and toss to coat. 2. Set the air fryer to 400°F (204°C). Spray the wings with oil. 3. Place the wings in the two baskets in a single layer and air fry for 20 to 25 minutes. Check with an instant-read thermometer and remove when they reach 155°F (68°C). Let rest until they reach 165°F (74°C). 4. While the wings are cooking, whisk together the avocado oil, hot sauce, butter, vinegar, and garlic in a small saucepan over medium-low heat until warm. 5. When the wings are done cooking, toss them with the Buffalo sauce. Serve warm.

Peruvian Chicken with Green Herb Sauce

Prep time: 30 minutes | Cook time: 15 minutes | Serves 4

Chicken:
4 boneless, skinless chicken thighs (about 1½ pounds / 680 g)
2 teaspoons grated lemon zest
2 tablespoons fresh lemon juice
1 tablespoon extra-virgin olive oil
1 serrano chile, seeded and minced
1 teaspoon ground cumin
½ teaspoon dried oregano, crushed
½ teaspoon kosher salt
Sauce:
1 cup fresh cilantro leaves
1 jalapeño, seeded and coarsely chopped
1 garlic clove, minced
1 tablespoon extra-virgin olive oil
2½ teaspoons fresh lime juice
¼ teaspoon kosher salt
⅓ cup mayonnaise

1. For the chicken: Use a fork to pierce the chicken all over to allow the marinade to penetrate better. In a small bowl, combine the lemon zest, lemon juice, olive oil, serrano, cumin, oregano, and salt. Place the chicken in a large bowl or large resealable plastic bag. Pour the marinade over the chicken. Toss to coat. Marinate at room temperature for 30 minutes, or cover and refrigerate for up to 24 hours. 2. Place the chicken in the two air fryer baskets. (Discard remaining marinade.) Set the air fryer to 350ºF (177ºC) for 15 minutes, turning halfway through the cooking time. 3. Meanwhile, for the sauce: Combine the cilantro, jalapeño, garlic, olive oil, lime juice, and salt in a blender. Blend until combined. Add the mayonnaise and blend until puréed. Transfer to a small bowl. Cover and chill until ready to serve. 4. At the end of the cooking time, use a meat thermometer to ensure the chicken has reached an internal temperature of 165ºF (74ºC). Serve the chicken with the sauce.

Quick Chicken Fajitas and Greek Chicken Souvlaki

Prep time: 30 minutes | Cook time: 15 minutes | Serves 5-6

Quick Chicken Fajitas:
10 ounces (283 g) boneless, skinless chicken breast, sliced into ¼-inch strips
2 tablespoons coconut oil, melted
1 tablespoon chili powder
½ teaspoon cumin
½ teaspoon paprika
½ teaspoon garlic powder
¼ medium onion, peeled and sliced
½ medium green bell pepper, seeded and sliced
½ medium red bell pepper, seeded and sliced
Greek Chicken Souvlaki:
Grated zest and juice of 1 lemon
2 tablespoons extra-virgin olive oil
1 tablespoon Greek souvlaki seasoning
1 pound (454 g) boneless, skinless chicken breast, cut into 2-inch chunks
Vegetable oil spray

Make the Quick Chicken Fajitas (zone 1 basket): 1. Place chicken and coconut oil into a large bowl and sprinkle with chili powder, cumin, paprika, and garlic powder. Toss chicken until well coated with seasoning. Place chicken into the zone 1 air fryer basket. 2. Adjust the temperature to 350ºF (177ºC) and air fry for 15 minutes. 3. Add onion and peppers into the basket when the cooking time has 7 minutes remaining. 4. Toss the chicken two or three times during cooking. Vegetables should be tender and chicken fully cooked to at least 165ºF (74ºC) internal temperature when finished. Make the Greek Chicken Souvlaki (zone 2 basket): 1. For the chicken: In a small bowl, combine the lemon zest, lemon juice, olive oil, and souvlaki seasoning. Place the chicken in a gallon-size resealable plastic bag. Pour the marinade over chicken. Seal bag and massage to coat. Place the bag in a large bowl and marinate for 30 minutes, or cover and refrigerate up to 24 hours, turning the bag occasionally. 2. Place the chicken a single layer in the zone 2 air fryer basket. Set the temperature to 350ºF (177ºC) for 10 minutes, turning the chicken and spraying with a little vegetable oil spray halfway through the cooking time. Increase the air fryer temperature to 400ºF (204ºC) for 5 minutes to allow the chicken to crisp and brown a little. 3. Transfer the chicken to a serving platter and serve.

Yellow Curry Chicken Thighs with Peanuts

Prep time: 10 minutes | Cook time: 20 minutes | Serves 6

½ cup unsweetened full-fat coconut milk
2 tablespoons yellow curry paste
1 tablespoon minced fresh ginger
1 tablespoon minced garlic
1 teaspoon kosher salt
1 pound (454 g) boneless, skinless chicken thighs, halved crosswise
2 tablespoons chopped peanuts

1. In a large bowl, stir together the coconut milk, curry paste, ginger, garlic, and salt until well blended. Add the chicken; toss well to coat. Marinate at room temperature for 30 minutes, or cover and refrigerate for up to 24 hours. 2. Preheat the air fryer to 375ºF (191ºC). 3. Place the chicken (along with marinade) in a baking pan. Place the pan in the air fryer basket. Bake for 20 minutes, turning the chicken halfway through the cooking time. Use a meat thermometer to ensure the chicken has reached an internal temperature of 165ºF (74ºC). 4. Sprinkle the chicken with the chopped peanuts and serve.

Chicken Legs with Leeks

Prep time: 30 minutes | Cook time: 18 minutes | Serves 6

2 leeks, sliced
2 large-sized tomatoes, chopped
3 cloves garlic, minced
½ teaspoon dried oregano
6 chicken legs, boneless and skinless
½ teaspoon smoked cayenne pepper
2 tablespoons olive oil
A freshly ground nutmeg

1. In a mixing dish, thoroughly combine all ingredients, minus the leeks. Place in the refrigerator and let it marinate overnight. 2. Lay the leeks onto the bottom of the two air fryer baskets. Top with the chicken legs. 3. Roast chicken legs at 375ºF (191ºC) for 18 minutes, turning halfway through. Serve with hoisin sauce.

Chapter 6 Beef, Pork, and Lamb

Chapter 6 Beef, Pork, and Lamb

Easy Lamb Chops with Asparagus and Pigs in a Blanket

Prep time: 20 minutes | Cook time: 15 minutes | Serves 6

Easy Lamb Chops with Asparagus:
4 asparagus spears, trimmed
2 tablespoons olive oil, divided
1 pound (454 g) lamb chops
1 garlic clove, minced
2 teaspoons chopped fresh thyme, for serving
Salt and ground black pepper, to taste

Pigs in a Blanket:
½ cup shredded Mozzarella cheese
2 tablespoons blanched finely ground almond flour
1 ounce (28 g) full-fat cream cheese
2 (2-ounce / 57-g) beef smoked sausages
½ teaspoon sesame seeds

Make the Easy Lamb Chops with Asparagus (zone 1 basket): 1. Preheat the zone 1 air fryer basket to 400ºF (204ºC). Spritz the zone 1 air fryer basket with cooking spray. 2. On a large plate, brush the asparagus with 1 tablespoon olive oil, then sprinkle with salt. Set aside. 3. On a separate plate, brush the lamb chops with remaining olive oil and sprinkle with salt and ground black pepper. 4. Arrange the lamb chops in the preheated air fryer. Air fry for 10 minutes. 5. Flip the lamb chops and add the asparagus and garlic. Air fry for 5 more minutes or until the lamb is well browned and the asparagus is tender. 6. Serve them on a plate with thyme on top.
Make the Pigs in a Blanket (zone 2 basket): 1. Place Mozzarella, almond flour, and cream cheese in a large microwave-safe bowl. Microwave for 45 seconds and stir until smooth. Roll dough into a ball and cut in half. 2. Press each half out into a 4 × 5-inch rectangle. Roll one sausage up in each dough half and press seams closed. Sprinkle the top with sesame seeds. 3. Place each wrapped sausage into the zone 2 air fryer basket. 4. Adjust the temperature to 400ºC (204ºC) and air fry for 7 minutes. 5. The outside will be golden when completely cooked. Serve immediately.

Teriyaki Rump Steak and Italian Lamb Chops

Prep time: 10 minutes | Cook time: 13 minutes | Serves 5

Teriyaki Rump Steak:
½ pound (227 g) rump steak
⅓ cup teriyaki marinade
Fine sea salt and ground black pepper, to taste
Cooking spray

Italian Lamb Chops:
2 lamp chops
2 teaspoons Italian herbs
2 avocados
½ cup mayonnaise
1 tablespoon lemon juice

1. Toss the rump steak in a large bowl with teriyaki marinade. Wrap the bowl in plastic and refrigerate to marinate for at least an hour. 2. Preheat the air fryer to 400ºF (204ºC) and spritz the two baskets with cooking spray. 3. Discard the marinade and transfer the steak in the zone 1 air fryer basket. Spritz with cooking spray. 4. Season the lamb chops with the Italian herbs, then set aside for 5 minutes. Place the rack inside the zone 2 air fryer basket and put the chops on the rack . 5. In zone 1, air fry for 13 minutes or until well browned. Flip the steak halfway through. In zone 2, air fry for 12 minutes. 6. In the meantime, halve the avocados and open to remove the pits. Spoon the flesh into a blender. 7. Add the mayonnaise and lemon juice and pulse until a smooth consistency is achieved. 8. Serve the steak and lamp chops with the avocado mayo.

Chinese-Style Baby Back Ribs

Prep time: 30 minutes | Cook time: 30 minutes | Serves 4

1 tablespoon toasted sesame oil
1 tablespoon fermented black bean paste
1 tablespoon Shaoxing wine (rice cooking wine)
1 tablespoon dark soy sauce
1 tablespoon agave nectar or honey
1 teaspoon minced garlic
1 teaspoon minced fresh ginger
1 (1½-pound / 680-g) slab baby back ribs, cut into individual ribs

1. In a large bowl, stir together the sesame oil, black bean paste, wine, soy sauce, agave, garlic, and ginger. Add the ribs and toss well to coat. Marinate at room temperature for 30 minutes, or cover and refrigerate for up to 24 hours. 2. Place the ribs in the two air fryer baskets; discard the marinade. Set the air fryer to 350ºF (177ºC) for 30 minutes.

Chuck Kebab with Arugula

Prep time: 30 minutes | Cook time: 25 minutes | Serves 4

½ cup leeks, chopped
2 garlic cloves, smashed
2 pounds (907 g) ground chuck
Salt, to taste
¼ teaspoon ground black pepper, or more to taste
1 teaspoon cayenne pepper
½ teaspoon ground sumac
3 saffron threads
2 tablespoons loosely packed fresh continental parsley leaves
4 tablespoons tahini sauce
4 ounces (113 g) baby arugula
1 tomato, cut into slices

1. In a bowl, mix the chopped leeks, garlic, ground chuck, and spices; knead with your hands until everything is well incorporated. 2. Now, mound the beef mixture around a wooden skewer into a pointed-ended sausage. 3. Cook in the preheated air fryer at 360ºF (182ºC) for 25 minutes. Serve your kebab with the tahini sauce, baby arugula and tomato. Enjoy!

Reuben Beef Rolls with Thousand Island Sauce

Prep time: 15 minutes | Cook time: 10 minutes | Makes 10 rolls

½ pound (227 g) cooked corned beef, chopped
½ cup drained and chopped sauerkraut
1 (8-ounce / 227-g) package cream cheese, softened
½ cup shredded Swiss cheese
20 slices prosciutto
Cooking spray

Thousand Island Sauce:
¼ cup chopped dill pickles
¼ cup tomato sauce
¾ cup mayonnaise
Fresh thyme leaves, for garnish
2 tablespoons sugar
⅛ teaspoon fine sea salt
Ground black pepper, to taste

1. Preheat the air fryer to 400°F (204°C) and spritz with cooking spray. 2. Combine the beef, sauerkraut, cream cheese, and Swiss cheese in a large bowl. Stir to mix well. 3. Unroll a slice of prosciutto on a clean work surface, then top with another slice of prosciutto crosswise. Scoop up 4 tablespoons of the beef mixture in the center. 4. Fold the top slice sides over the filling as the ends of the roll, then roll up the long sides of the bottom prosciutto and make it into a roll shape. Overlap the sides by about 1 inch. Repeat with remaining filling and prosciutto. 5. Arrange the rolls in the preheated two air fryer baskets, seam side down, and spritz with cooking spray. 6. Air fry for 10 minutes or until golden and crispy. Flip the rolls halfway through. 7. Meanwhile, combine the ingredients for the sauce in a small bowl. Stir to mix well. 8. Serve the rolls with the dipping sauce.

Greek Lamb Pita Pockets

Prep time: 15 minutes | Cook time: 6 minutes | Serves 4

Dressing:
1 cup plain yogurt
1 tablespoon lemon juice
1 teaspoon dried dill weed, crushed
1 teaspoon ground oregano
½ teaspoon salt
Meatballs:
½ pound (227 g) ground lamb
1 tablespoon diced onion
1 teaspoon dried parsley
1 teaspoon dried dill weed, crushed

¼ teaspoon oregano
¼ teaspoon coriander
¼ teaspoon ground cumin
¼ teaspoon salt
4 pita halves
Suggested Toppings:
1 red onion, slivered
1 medium cucumber, deseeded, thinly sliced
Crumbled feta cheese
Sliced black olives
Chopped fresh peppers

1. Preheat the zone 1 air fryer basket to 390°F (199°C). 2. Stir the dressing ingredients together in a small bowl and refrigerate while preparing lamb. 3. Combine all meatball ingredients in a large bowl and stir to distribute seasonings. 4. Shape meat mixture into 12 small meatballs, rounded or slightly flattened if you prefer. 5. Transfer the meatballs in the preheated zone 1 air fryer basket and air fry for 6 minutes, until well done. Remove and drain on paper towels. 6. To serve, pile meatballs and the choice of toppings in pita pockets and drizzle with dressing.

Chorizo and Beef Burger

Prep time: 10 minutes | Cook time: 15 minutes | Serves 4

¾ pound (340 g) 80/20 ground beef
¼ pound (113 g) Mexican-style ground chorizo
¼ cup chopped onion

5 slices pickled jalapeños, chopped
2 teaspoons chili powder
1 teaspoon minced garlic
¼ teaspoon cumin

1. In a large bowl, mix all ingredients. Divide the mixture into four sections and form them into burger patties. 2. Place burger patties into the two air fryer baskets. 3. Adjust the temperature to 375°F (191°C) and air fry for 15 minutes. 4. Flip the patties halfway through the cooking time. Serve warm.

Parmesan Herb Filet Mignon

Prep time: 20 minutes | Cook time: 13 minutes | Serves 4

1 pound (454 g) filet mignon
Sea salt and ground black pepper, to taste
½ teaspoon cayenne pepper
1 teaspoon dried basil

1 teaspoon dried rosemary
1 teaspoon dried thyme
1 tablespoon sesame oil
1 small-sized egg, well-whisked
½ cup Parmesan cheese, grated

1. Season the filet mignon with salt, black pepper, cayenne pepper, basil, rosemary, and thyme. Brush with sesame oil. 2. Put the egg in a shallow plate. Now, place the Parmesan cheese in another plate. 3. Coat the filet mignon with the egg; then lay it into the Parmesan cheese. Set the air fryer to 360°F (182°C). 4. Cook for 10 to 13 minutes or until golden. Serve with mixed salad leaves and enjoy!

Tenderloin with Crispy Shallots

Prep time: 30 minutes | Cook time: 18 to 20 minutes | Serves 6

1½ pounds (680 g) beef tenderloin steaks
Sea salt and freshly ground black pepper, to taste

4 medium shallots
1 teaspoon olive oil or avocado oil

1. Season both sides of the steaks with salt and pepper, and let them sit at room temperature for 45 minutes. 2. Set the air fryer to 400°F (204°C) and let it preheat for 5 minutes. 3. Place the steaks in the two air fryer baskets in a single layer and air fry for 5 minutes. Flip and cook for 5 minutes longer, until an instant-read thermometer inserted in the center of the steaks registers 120°F (49°C) for medium-rare (or as desired). Remove the steaks and tent with aluminum foil to rest. 4. Set the air fryer to 300°F (149°C). In a medium bowl, toss the shallots with the oil. Place the shallots in the basket and air fry for 5 minutes, then give them a toss and cook for 3 to 5 minutes more, until crispy and golden brown. 5. Place the steaks on serving plates and arrange the shallots on top.

Blackened Steak Nuggets and Beef Loin with Thyme and Parsley

Prep time: 15 minutes | Cook time: 15 minutes | Serves 6

Blackened Steak Nuggets:
1 pound (454 g) rib eye steak, cut into 1-inch cubes
2 tablespoons salted butter, melted
½ teaspoon paprika
½ teaspoon salt
¼ teaspoon garlic powder
¼ teaspoon onion powder
¼ teaspoon ground black pepper
⅛ teaspoon cayenne pepper

Beef Loin with Thyme and Parsley:
1 tablespoon butter, melted
¼ dried thyme
1 teaspoon garlic salt
¼ teaspoon dried parsley
1 pound (454 g) beef loin

Make the Blackened Steak Nuggets (zone 1 basket): 1. Place steak into a large bowl and pour in butter. Toss to coat. Sprinkle with remaining ingredients. 2. Place bites into the ungreased zone 1 air fryer basket. Adjust the temperature to 400ºF (204ºC) and air fry for 7 minutes, shaking the basket three times during cooking. Steak will be crispy on the outside and browned when done and internal temperature is at least 150ºF (66ºC) for medium and 180ºF (82ºC) for well-done. Serve warm.
Make the Beef Loin with Thyme and Parsley (zone 2 basket): 1. Preheat the zone 2 air fryer basket to 400ºF (204ºC). 2. In a bowl, combine the melted butter, thyme, garlic salt, and parsley. 3. Cut the beef loin into slices and generously apply the seasoned butter using a brush. Transfer to the zone 2 air fryer basket. 4. Air fry the beef for 15 minutes. 5. Take care when removing it and serve hot.

Swedish Meatballs

Prep time: 25 minutes | Cook time: 20 minutes | Serves 4

Meatballs:
¾ cup fresh bread crumbs
¼ cup heavy cream
¼ cup finely chopped onion
½ teaspoon dried parsley flakes
½ teaspoon kosher salt
¼ teaspoon ground allspice
¼ teaspoon freshly grated nutmeg
¼ teaspoon white pepper
½ pound (227 g) 85% lean ground beef
½ pound (227 g) ground pork
1 large egg, beaten
1 egg white, lightly beaten

Gravy:
2 tablespoons salted butter
2 tablespoons all-purpose flour
1½ cups low-sodium beef broth
1 teaspoon Worcestershire sauce
¼ cup heavy cream
Kosher salt and black pepper, to taste

For Serving:
Chopped fresh parsley
Lingonberry jam

1. For the meatballs: In a large bowl, mix the bread crumbs and cream until well combined; let stand for 5 minutes. Add the onion, parsley flakes, salt, allspice, nutmeg, and white pepper. Stir to make a thick paste. Add the ground beef, ground pork, egg, and egg white. Mix until evenly combined. 2. Form into 1-inch meatballs. Place in a single layer in the two air fryer baskets. Set the air fryer to 350ºF (177ºC) for 20 minutes, turning halfway through the cooking time. 3. Meanwhile, for the gravy: In a medium saucepan, melt the butter over medium heat. Add the flour and cook, whisking, until smooth. Whisk in the broth and Worcestershire. Bring to a simmer. Add the cream. Reduce the heat to medium-low and simmer until the gravy thickens, about 10 minutes. Season with salt and black pepper. 4. At the end of the cooking time, use a meat thermometer to ensure the meatballs have reached an internal temperature of 160ºF / 71ºC (medium). 5. Transfer the meatballs to a serving bowl. Ladle the gravy over the meatballs and sprinkle with parsley. Serve with lingonberry jam.

Pork Milanese

Prep time: 10 minutes | Cook time: 12 minutes | Serves 4

4 (1-inch) boneless pork chops
Fine sea salt and ground black pepper, to taste
2 large eggs
¾ cup powdered Parmesan cheese
Chopped fresh parsley, for garnish
Lemon slices, for serving

1. Spray the air fryer basket with avocado oil. Preheat the air fryer to 400ºF (204ºC). 2. Place the pork chops between 2 sheets of plastic wrap and pound them with the flat side of a meat tenderizer until they're ¼ inch thick. Lightly season both sides of the chops with salt and pepper. 3. Lightly beat the eggs in a shallow bowl. Divide the Parmesan cheese evenly between 2 bowls and set the bowls in this order: Parmesan, eggs, Parmesan. Dredge a chop in the first bowl of Parmesan, then dip it in the eggs, and then dredge it again in the second bowl of Parmesan, making sure both sides and all edges are well coated. Repeat with the remaining chops. 4. Place the chops in the two air fryer baskets and air fry for 12 minutes, or until the internal temperature reaches 145ºF (63ºC), flipping halfway through. 5. Garnish with fresh parsley and serve immediately with lemon slices. Store leftovers in an airtight container in the refrigerator for up to 3 days. Reheat in a preheated 390ºF (199ºC) air fryer for 5 minutes, or until warmed through.

Korean Beef Tacos

Prep time: 30 minutes | Cook time: 12 minutes | Serves 6

2 tablespoons gochujang (Korean red chile paste)
2 cloves garlic, minced
2 teaspoons minced fresh ginger
2 tablespoons toasted sesame oil
1 tablespoon soy sauce
2 tablespoons sesame seeds
2 teaspoons sugar
½ teaspoon kosher salt
1½ pounds (680 g) thinly sliced beef (chuck, rib eye, or sirloin)
1 medium red onion, sliced
12 (6-inch) flour tortillas, warmed; or lettuce leaves
½ cup chopped green onions
¼ cup chopped fresh cilantro (optional)
½ cup kimchi (optional)

1. In a small bowl, combine the gochujang, garlic, ginger, sesame oil, soy sauce, sesame seeds, sugar, and salt. Whisk until well combined. Place the beef and red onion in a resealable plastic bag and pour the marinade over. Seal the bag and massage to coat all of the meat and onion. Marinate at room temperature for 30 minutes or in the refrigerator for up to 24 hours. 2. Place the meat and onion in the two air fryer baskets, leaving behind as much of the marinade as possible; discard the marinade. Set the air fryer to 400ºF (204ºC) for 12 minutes, shaking halfway through the cooking time. 3. To serve, place meat and onion in the tortillas. Top with the green onions and the cilantro and kimchi, if using, and serve.

Beef and Goat Cheese Stuffed Peppers

Prep time: 10 minutes | Cook time: 30 minutes | Serves 4

1 pound (454 g) lean ground beef	1 teaspoon salt
½ cup cooked brown rice	½ teaspoon black pepper
2 Roma tomatoes, diced	¼ teaspoon ground allspice
3 garlic cloves, minced	2 bell peppers, halved and seeded
½ yellow onion, diced	4 ounces (113 g) goat cheese
2 tablespoons fresh oregano, chopped	¼ cup fresh parsley, chopped

1. Preheat the air fryer to 360°F(182°C). 2. In a large bowl, combine the ground beef, rice, tomatoes, garlic, onion, oregano, salt, pepper, and allspice. Mix well. 3. Divide the beef mixture equally into the halved bell peppers and top each with about 1 ounce (28 g a quarter of the total) of the goat cheese. 4. Place the peppers into the zone 1 air fryer basket in a single layer, making sure that they don't touch each other. Bake for 30 minutes. 5. Remove the peppers from the air fryer and top with fresh parsley before serving.

Jalapeño Popper Pork Chops

Prep time: 15 minutes | Cook time: 6 to 8 minutes | Serves 4

1¾ pounds (794 g) bone-in, center-cut loin pork chops	4 ounces (113 g) sliced bacon, cooked and crumbled
Sea salt and freshly ground black pepper, to taste	4 ounces (113 g) Cheddar cheese, shredded
6 ounces (170 g) cream cheese, at room temperature	1 jalapeño, seeded and diced
	1 teaspoon garlic powder

1. Cut a pocket into each pork chop, lengthwise along the side, making sure not to cut it all the way through. Season the outside of the chops with salt and pepper. 2. In a small bowl, combine the cream cheese, bacon, Cheddar cheese, jalapeño, and garlic powder. Divide this mixture among the pork chops, stuffing it into the pocket of each chop. 3. Set the air fryer to 400°F (204°C). Place the pork chops in the two air fryer baskets in a single layer. Air fry for 3 minutes. Flip the chops and cook for 3 to 5 minutes more, until an instant-read thermometer reads 145°F (63°C). 4. Allow the chops to rest for 5 minutes, then serve warm.

Cinnamon-Beef Kofta

Prep time: 10 minutes | Cook time: 13 minutes | Makes 12 koftas

1½ pounds (680 g) lean ground beef	1 teaspoon ground cumin
1 teaspoon onion powder	¾ teaspoon salt
¾ teaspoon ground cinnamon	¼ teaspoon cayenne
¾ teaspoon ground dried turmeric	12 (3½- to 4-inch-long) cinnamon sticks
	Cooking spray

1. Preheat the air fryer to 375°F (191°C). Spritz the two air fryer baskets with cooking spray. 2. Combine all the ingredients, except for the cinnamon sticks, in a large bowl. Toss to mix well. 3. Divide and shape the mixture into 12 balls, then wrap each ball around each cinnamon stick and leave a quarter of the length uncovered. 4. Arrange the beef-cinnamon sticks in the preheated air fryer and spritz with cooking spray. 5. Air fry for 13 minutes or until the beef is browned. Flip the sticks halfway through. 6. Serve immediately.

Pork and Beef Egg Rolls

Prep time: 30 minutes | Cook time: 7 to 8 minutes | Makes 8 egg rolls

¼ pound (113 g) very lean ground beef	¼ cup chopped water chestnuts
¼ pound (113 g) lean ground pork	¼ teaspoon salt
1 tablespoon soy sauce	¼ teaspoon garlic powder
1 teaspoon olive oil	¼ teaspoon black pepper
½ cup grated carrots	1 egg
2 green onions, chopped	1 tablespoon water
2 cups grated Napa cabbage	8 egg roll wraps
	Oil for misting or cooking spray

1. In a large skillet, brown beef and pork with soy sauce. Remove cooked meat from skillet, drain, and set aside. 2. Pour off any excess grease from skillet. Add olive oil, carrots, and onions. Sauté until barely tender, about 1 minute. 3. Stir in cabbage, cover, and cook for 1 minute or just until cabbage slightly wilts. Remove from heat. 4. In a large bowl, combine the cooked meats and vegetables, water chestnuts, salt, garlic powder, and pepper. Stir well. If needed, add more salt to taste. 5. Beat together egg and water in a small bowl. 6. Fill egg roll wrappers, using about ¼ cup of filling for each wrap. Roll up and brush all over with egg wash to seal. Spray very lightly with olive oil or cooking spray. 7. Place 8 egg rolls in the two air fryer baskets and air fry at 390°F (199°C) for 4 minutes. Turn over and cook 3 to 4 more minutes, until golden brown and crispy.

Herbed Lamb Steaks

Prep time: 30 minutes | Cook time: 15 minutes | Serves 4

½ medium onion	1 teaspoon cayenne pepper
2 tablespoons minced garlic	1 teaspoon salt
2 teaspoons ground ginger	4 (6-ounce / 170-g) boneless lamb sirloin steaks
1 teaspoon ground cinnamon	
1 teaspoon onion powder	Oil, for spraying

1. In a blender, combine the onion, garlic, ginger, cinnamon, onion powder, cayenne pepper, and salt and pulse until the onion is minced. 2. Place the lamb steaks in a large bowl or zip-top plastic bag and sprinkle the onion mixture over the top. Turn the steaks until they are evenly coated. Cover with plastic wrap or seal the bag and refrigerate for 30 minutes. 3. Preheat the air fryer to 330°F (166°C). Line the two air fryer baskets with parchment and spray lightly with oil. 4. Place the lamb steaks in a single layer in the prepared baskets, making sure they don't overlap. 5. Cook for 8 minutes, flip, and cook for another 7 minutes, or until the internal temperature reaches 155°F (68°C).

London Broil with Herb Butter

Prep time: 30 minutes | Cook time: 20 to 25 minutes | Serves 4

1½ pounds (680 g) London broil top round steak
¼ cup olive oil
2 tablespoons balsamic vinegar
1 tablespoon Worcestershire sauce
4 cloves garlic, minced
Herb Butter:
6 tablespoons unsalted butter, softened
1 tablespoon chopped fresh parsley
¼ teaspoon salt
¼ teaspoon dried ground rosemary or thyme
¼ teaspoon garlic powder
Pinch of red pepper flakes

1. Place the beef in a gallon-size resealable bag. In a small bowl, whisk together the olive oil, balsamic vinegar, Worcestershire sauce, and garlic. Pour the marinade over the beef, massaging gently to coat, and seal the bag. Let sit at room temperature for an hour or refrigerate overnight. 2. To make the herb butter: In a small bowl, mix the butter with the parsley, salt, rosemary, garlic powder, and red pepper flakes until smooth. Cover and refrigerate until ready to use. 3. Preheat the air fryer to 400°F (204°C). 4. Remove the beef from the marinade (discard the marinade) and place the beef in the two air fryer baskets. Pausing halfway through the cooking time to turn the meat, air fry for 20 to 25 minutes, until a thermometer inserted into the thickest part indicates the desired doneness, 125°F / 52°C (rare) to 150°F / 66°C (medium). Let the beef rest for 10 minutes before slicing. Serve topped with the herb butter.

Marinated Steak Tips with Mushrooms

Prep time: 30 minutes | Cook time: 10 minutes | Serves 4

1½ pounds (680 g) sirloin, trimmed and cut into 1-inch pieces
8 ounces (227 g) brown mushrooms, halved
¼ cup Worcestershire sauce
1 tablespoon Dijon mustard
1 tablespoon olive oil
1 teaspoon paprika
1 teaspoon crushed red pepper flakes
2 tablespoons chopped fresh parsley (optional)

1. Place the beef and mushrooms in a gallon-size resealable bag. In a small bowl, whisk together the Worcestershire, mustard, olive oil, paprika, and red pepper flakes. Pour the marinade into the bag and massage gently to ensure the beef and mushrooms are evenly coated. Seal the bag and refrigerate for at least 4 hours, preferably overnight. Remove from the refrigerator 30 minutes before cooking. 2. Preheat the air fryer to 400°F (204°C). 3. Drain and discard the marinade. Arrange the steak and mushrooms in the two air fryer baskets. Air fry for 10 minutes, pausing halfway through the baking time to shake the basket. Transfer to a serving plate and top with the parsley, if desired.

Spice-Rubbed Pork Loin

Prep time: 5 minutes | Cook time: 20 minutes | Serves 6

1 teaspoon paprika
½ teaspoon ground cumin
½ teaspoon chili powder
½ teaspoon garlic powder
2 tablespoons coconut oil
1 (1½-pound / 680-g) boneless pork loin
½ teaspoon salt
¼ teaspoon ground black pepper

1. In a small bowl, mix paprika, cumin, chili powder, and garlic powder. 2. Drizzle coconut oil over pork. Sprinkle pork loin with salt and pepper, then rub spice mixture evenly on all sides. 3. Place pork loin into the two ungreased air fryer baskets. Adjust the temperature to 400°F (204°C) and air fry for 20 minutes, turning pork halfway through cooking. Pork loin will be browned and have an internal temperature of at least 145°F (63°C) when done. Serve warm.

Parmesan-Crusted Steak

Prep time: 30 minutes | Cook time: 12 minutes | Serves 6

½ cup (1 stick) unsalted butter, at room temperature
1 cup finely grated Parmesan cheese
¼ cup finely ground blanched almond flour
1½ pounds (680 g) New York strip steak
Sea salt and freshly ground black pepper, to taste

1. Place the butter, Parmesan cheese, and almond flour in a food processor. Process until smooth. Transfer to a sheet of parchment paper and form into a log. Wrap tightly in plastic wrap. Freeze for 45 minutes or refrigerate for at least 4 hours. 2. While the butter is chilling, season the steak liberally with salt and pepper. Let the steak rest at room temperature for about 45 minutes. 3. Place the two baskets in your air fryer, set it to 400°F (204°C), and let it preheat for 5 minutes. 4. Place the steak on the baskets and air fry for 4 minutes. Flip and cook for 3 minutes more, until the steak is brown on both sides. 5. Remove the steak from the air fryer and arrange an equal amount of the Parmesan butter on top of each steak. Return the steak to the air fryer and continue cooking for another 5 minutes, until an instant-read thermometer reads 120°F (49°C) for medium-rare and the crust is golden brown (or to your desired doneness). 6. Transfer the cooked steak to a plate; let rest for 10 minutes before serving.

Chapter 7 Snacks and Appetizers

Chapter 7 Snacks and Appetizers

Crunchy Tex-Mex Tortilla Chips

Prep time: 5 minutes | Cook time: 5 minutes | Serves 4

Olive oil
½ teaspoon salt
½ teaspoon ground cumin
½ teaspoon chili powder
½ teaspoon paprika
Pinch cayenne pepper
8 (6-inch) corn tortillas, each cut into 6 wedges

1. Spray the two air fryer baskets lightly with olive oil. 2. In a small bowl, combine the salt, cumin, chili powder, paprika, and cayenne pepper. 3. Place the tortilla wedges in the two air fryer baskets in a single layer. Spray the tortillas lightly with oil and sprinkle with some of the seasoning mixture. 4. Air fry at 375°F (191°C) for 2 to 3 minutes. Shake the baskets and cook until the chips are light brown and crispy, an additional 2 to 3 minutes. Watch the chips closely so they do not burn.

String Bean Fries and Spiced Roasted Cashews

Prep time: 20 minutes | Cook time: 10 minutes | Serves 8

String Bean Fries:
½ pound (227 g) fresh string beans
2 eggs
4 teaspoons water
½ cup white flour
½ cup bread crumbs
¼ teaspoon salt
¼ teaspoon ground black pepper
¼ teaspoon dry mustard (optional)
Oil for misting or cooking spray
Spiced Roasted Cashews:
2 cups raw cashews
2 tablespoons olive oil
¼ teaspoon salt
¼ teaspoon chili powder
⅛ teaspoon garlic powder
⅛ teaspoon smoked paprika

Make the String Bean Fries (zone 1 basket): 1. Preheat the air fryer to 360°F (182°C). 2. Trim stem ends from string beans, wash, and pat dry. 3. In a shallow dish, beat eggs and water together until well blended. 4. Place flour in a second shallow dish. 5. In a third shallow dish, stir together the bread crumbs, salt, pepper, and dry mustard if using. 6. Dip each string bean in egg mixture, flour, egg mixture again, then bread crumbs. 7. When you finish coating all the string beans, place them in the zone 1 basket. 8. Cook for 3 minutes. 9. Stop and mist string beans with oil or cooking spray. 10. Cook for 2 to 3 more minutes or until string beans are crispy and nicely browned.
Make the Spiced Roasted Cashews (zone 2 basket): 1. Preheat the air fryer to 360°F (182°C). 2. In a large bowl, toss all of the ingredients together. 3. Pour the cashews into the zone 2 air fryer basket and roast them for 5 minutes. Shake the basket, then cook for 5 minutes more. 4. Serve immediately.

Hush Puppies

Prep time: 45 minutes | Cook time: 10 minutes | Serves 12

1 cup self-rising yellow cornmeal
½ cup all-purpose flour
1 teaspoon sugar
1 teaspoon salt
1 teaspoon freshly ground black pepper
1 large egg
⅓ cup canned creamed corn
1 cup minced onion
2 teaspoons minced jalapeño pepper
2 tablespoons olive oil, divided

1. Thoroughly combine the cornmeal, flour, sugar, salt, and pepper in a large bowl. 2. Whisk together the egg and corn in a small bowl. Pour the egg mixture into the bowl of cornmeal mixture and stir to combine. Stir in the minced onion and jalapeño. Cover the bowl with plastic wrap and place in the refrigerator for 30 minutes. 3. Preheat the air fryer to 375°F (191°C). Line the two air fryer baskets with parchment paper and lightly brush it with 1 tablespoon of olive oil. 4. Scoop out the cornmeal mixture and form into 24 balls, about 1 inch. 5. Arrange the balls in the parchment paper-lined basket, leaving space between each ball. 6. Air fry for 5 minutes. Shake the baskets and brush the balls with the remaining 1 tablespoon of olive oil. Continue cooking for 5 minutes until golden brown. 7. Remove the balls (hush puppies) from the baskets and serve on a plate.

Crispy Phyllo Artichoke Triangles

Prep time: 15 minutes | Cook time: 9 to 12 minutes | Makes 18 triangles

¼ cup Ricotta cheese
1 egg white
⅓ cup minced and drained artichoke hearts
3 tablespoons grated Mozzarella cheese
½ teaspoon dried thyme
6 sheets frozen phyllo dough, thawed
2 tablespoons melted butter

1. Preheat the air fryer to 400°F (204°C). 2. In a small bowl, combine the Ricotta cheese, egg white, artichoke hearts, Mozzarella cheese, and thyme, and mix well. 3. Cover the phyllo dough with a damp kitchen towel while you work so it doesn't dry out. Using one sheet at a time, place on the work surface and cut into thirds lengthwise. 4. Put about 1½ teaspoons of the filling on each strip at the base. Fold the bottom right-hand tip of phyllo over the filling to meet the other side in a triangle, then continue folding in a triangle. Brush each triangle with butter to seal the edges. Repeat with the remaining phyllo dough and filling. 5. Place the triangles in the two air fryer baskets. Bake, 6 at a time in a basket, for about 3 to 4 minutes, or until the phyllo is golden brown and crisp. 6. Serve hot.

Roasted Mushrooms with Garlic and Lebanese Muhammara

Prep time: 18 minutes | Cook time: 22 to 27 minutes | Serves 9

Roasted Mushrooms with Garlic:
16 garlic cloves, peeled
2 teaspoons olive oil, divided
16 button mushrooms
½ teaspoon dried marjoram
⅛ teaspoon freshly ground black pepper
1 tablespoon white wine or low-sodium vegetable broth
Lebanese Muhammara:
2 large red bell peppers
¼ cup plus 2 tablespoons extra-virgin olive oil
1 cup walnut halves
1 tablespoon agave nectar or honey
1 teaspoon fresh lemon juice
1 teaspoon ground cumin
1 teaspoon kosher salt
1 teaspoon red pepper flakes
Raw vegetables (such as cucumber, carrots, zucchini slices, or cauliflower) or toasted pita chips, for serving

Roasted Mushrooms with Garlic (zone 1 basket): 1. In a baking pan, mix the garlic with 1 teaspoon of olive oil. Roast in the zone 1 air fryer basket at 350°F (177°C) for 12 minutes. 2. Add the mushrooms, marjoram, and pepper. Stir to coat. Drizzle with the remaining 1 teaspoon of olive oil and the white wine. 3. Return to the air fryer basket and roast for 10 to 15 minutes more, or until the mushrooms and garlic cloves are tender. Serve.
Lebanese Muhammara (zone 2 basket): 1. Drizzle the peppers with 2 tablespoons of the olive oil and place in the zone 2 air fryer basket. Set the temperature to 400°F (204°C) for 10 minutes. 2. Add the walnuts to the basket, arranging them around the peppers. Set the temperature to 400°F (204°C) for 5 minutes. 3. Remove the peppers, seal in a resealable plastic bag, and let rest for 5 to 10 minutes. Transfer the walnuts to a plate and set aside to cool. 4. Place the softened peppers, walnuts, agave, lemon juice, cumin, salt, and ½ teaspoon of the pepper flakes in a food processor and purée until smooth. 5. Transfer the dip to a serving bowl and make an indentation in the middle. Pour the remaining ¼ cup olive oil into the indentation. Garnish the dip with the remaining ½ teaspoon pepper flakes. 6. Serve with vegetables or toasted pita chips.

Greek Street Tacos

Prep time: 10 minutes | Cook time: 3 minutes | Makes 8 small tacos

8 small flour tortillas (4-inch diameter)
8 tablespoons hummus
4 tablespoons crumbled feta cheese
4 tablespoons chopped kalamata or other olives (optional)
Olive oil for misting

1. Place 1 tablespoon of hummus or tapenade in the center of each tortilla. Top with 1 teaspoon of feta crumbles and 1 teaspoon of chopped olives, if using. 2. Using your finger or a small spoon, moisten the edges of the tortilla all around with water. 3. Fold tortilla over to make a half-moon shape. Press center gently. Then press the edges firmly to seal in the filling. 4. Mist both sides with olive oil. 5. Place in the two air fryer baskets, very close but try not to overlap. 6. Air fry at 390°F (199°C) for 3 minutes, just until lightly browned and crispy.

Crunchy Chickpeas and Beef and Mango Skewers

Prep time: 15 minutes | Cook time: 15 to 20 minutes | Serves 8

Crunchy Chickpeas:
½ teaspoon chili powder
½ teaspoon ground cumin
¼ teaspoon cayenne pepper
¼ teaspoon salt
1 (19-ounce / 539-g) can chickpeas, drained and rinsed
Cooking spray
Beef and Mango Skewers:
¾ pound (340 g) beef sirloin tip, cut into 1-inch cubes
2 tablespoons balsamic vinegar
1 tablespoon olive oil
1 tablespoon honey
½ teaspoon dried marjoram
Pinch of salt
Freshly ground black pepper, to taste
1 mango

Make the Crunchy Chickpeas (zone 1 basket): 1. Preheat the air fryer to 390°F (199°C). Lightly spritz the zone 1 air fryer basket with cooking spray. 2. Mix the chili powder, cumin, cayenne pepper, and salt in a small bowl. 3. Place the chickpeas in a medium bowl and lightly mist with cooking spray. 4. Add the spice mixture to the chickpeas and toss until evenly coated. 5. Place the chickpeas in the zone 1 air fryer basket and air fry for 15 to 20 minutes, or until the chickpeas are cooked to your preferred crunchiness. Shake the basket three or four times during cooking. 6. Let the chickpeas cool for 5 minutes before serving.
Make the Beef and Mango Skewers (zone 2 basket): 1. Preheat the air fryer to 390°F (199°C). 2. Put the beef cubes in a medium bowl and add the balsamic vinegar, olive oil, honey, marjoram, salt, and pepper. Mix well, then massage the marinade into the beef with your hands. Set aside. 3. To prepare the mango, stand it on end and cut the skin off, using a sharp knife. Then carefully cut around the oval pit to remove the flesh. Cut the mango into 1-inch cubes. 4. Thread metal skewers alternating with three beef cubes and two mango cubes. 5. Roast the skewers in the zone 2 air fryer basket for 4 to 7 minutes, or until the beef is browned and at least 145°F (63°C). 6. Serve hot.

Cheesy Zucchini Tots

Prep time: 15 minutes | Cook time: 6 minutes | Serves 8

2 medium zucchini (about 12 ounces / 340 g), shredded
1 large egg, whisked
½ cup grated pecorino romano cheese
½ cup panko bread crumbs
¼ teaspoon black pepper
1 clove garlic, minced
Cooking spray

1. Using your hands, squeeze out as much liquid from the zucchini as possible. In a large bowl, mix the zucchini with the remaining ingredients except the oil until well incorporated. 2. Make the zucchini tots: Use a spoon or cookie scoop to place tablespoonfuls of the zucchini mixture onto a lightly floured cutting board and form into 1-inch logs. 3. Preheat air fryer to 375°F (191°C). Spritz the two air fryer baskets with cooking spray. 4. Place the tots in the two baskets. 5. Air fry for 6 minutes until golden brown. 6. Remove from the baskets to a serving plate and repeat with the remaining zucchini tots. 7. Serve immediately.

Fried Artichoke Hearts

Prep time: 10 minutes | Cook time: 12 minutes | Serves 10

Oil, for spraying
3 (14-ounce / 397-g) cans quartered artichokes, drained and patted dry
½ cup mayonnaise
1 cup panko bread crumbs
⅓ cup grated Parmesan cheese
Salt and freshly ground black pepper, to taste

1. Line the two air fryer baskets with parchment and spray lightly with oil. 2. Place the artichokes on a plate. Put the mayonnaise and bread crumbs in separate bowls. 3. Working one at a time, dredge each artichoke piece in the mayonnaise, then in the bread crumbs to cover. 4. Place the artichokes in the prepared baskets. 5. Air fry at 370°F (188°C) for 10 to 12 minutes, or until crispy and golden brown. 6. Sprinkle with the Parmesan cheese and season with salt and black pepper. Serve immediately.

Greens Chips with Curried Yogurt Sauce

Prep time: 10 minutes | Cook time: 5 to 6 minutes | Serves 4

1 cup low-fat Greek yogurt
1 tablespoon freshly squeezed lemon juice
1 tablespoon curry powder
½ bunch curly kale, stemmed, ribs removed and discarded, leaves cut into 2- to 3-inch pieces
½ bunch chard, stemmed, ribs removed and discarded, leaves cut into 2- to 3-inch pieces
1½ teaspoons olive oil

1. In a small bowl, stir together the yogurt, lemon juice, and curry powder. Set aside. 2. In a large bowl, toss the kale and chard with the olive oil, working the oil into the leaves with your hands. This helps break up the fibers in the leaves so the chips are tender. 3. Air fry the greens in the two air fryer baskets at 390°F (199°C) for 5 to 6 minutes, until crisp, shaking the baskets once during cooking. Serve with the yogurt sauce.

Mozzarella Arancini

Prep time: 5 minutes | Cook time: 8 to 11 minutes | Makes 16 arancini

2 cups cooked rice, cooled
2 eggs, beaten
1½ cups panko bread crumbs, divided
½ cup grated Parmesan cheese
2 tablespoons minced fresh basil
16 ¾-inch cubes Mozzarella cheese
2 tablespoons olive oil

1. Preheat the air fryer to 400°F (204°C). 2. In a medium bowl, combine the rice, eggs, ½ cup of the bread crumbs, Parmesan cheese, and basil. Form this mixture into 16 1½-inch balls. 3. Poke a hole in each of the balls with your finger and insert a Mozzarella cube. Form the rice mixture firmly around the cheese. 4. On a shallow plate, combine the remaining 1 cup of the bread crumbs with the olive oil and mix well. Roll the rice balls in the bread crumbs to coat. 5. Air fry the arancini in the two air fryer baskets for 8 to 11 minutes or until golden brown. 6. Serve hot.

Spinach and Crab Meat Cups

Prep time: 10 minutes | Cook time: 10 minutes | Makes 30 cups

1 (6-ounce / 170-g) can crab meat, drained to yield ⅓ cup meat
¼ cup frozen spinach, thawed, drained, and chopped
1 clove garlic, minced
½ cup grated Parmesan cheese
3 tablespoons plain yogurt
¼ teaspoon lemon juice
½ teaspoon Worcestershire sauce
30 mini frozen phyllo shells, thawed
Cooking spray

1. Preheat the air fryer to 390°F (199°C). 2. Remove any bits of shell that might remain in the crab meat. 3. Mix the crab meat, spinach, garlic, and cheese together. 4. Stir in the yogurt, lemon juice, and Worcestershire sauce and mix well. 5. Spoon a teaspoon of filling into each phyllo shell. 6. Spray the two air fryer baskets with cooking spray and arrange shells in the baskets. Air fry for 5 minutes. 7. Serve immediately.

Pickle Chips

Prep time: 30 minutes | Cook time: 12 minutes | Serves 4

Oil, for spraying
2 cups sliced dill or sweet pickles, drained
1 cup buttermilk
2 cups all-purpose flour
2 large eggs, beaten
2 cups panko bread crumbs
¼ teaspoon salt

1. Line the two air fryer baskets with parchment and spray lightly with oil. 2. In a shallow bowl, combine the pickles and buttermilk and let soak for at least 1 hour, then drain. 3. Place the flour, beaten eggs, and bread crumbs in separate bowls. 4. Coat each pickle chip lightly in the flour, dip in the eggs, and dredge in the bread crumbs. Be sure each one is evenly coated. 5. Place the pickle chips in the prepared baskets, sprinkle with the salt, and spray lightly with oil. 6. Air fry at 390°F (199°C) for 5 minutes, flip, and cook for another 5 to 7 minutes, or until crispy. Serve hot.

Skinny Fries

Prep time: 10 minutes | Cook time: 15 minutes | Serves 3

2 to 3 russet potatoes, peeled and cut into ¼-inch sticks
2 to 3 teaspoons olive or vegetable oil
Salt, to taste

1. Cut the potatoes into ¼-inch strips. (A mandolin with a julienne blade is really helpful here.) Rinse the potatoes with cold water several times and let them soak in cold water for at least 10 minutes or as long as overnight. 2. Preheat the air fryer to 380°F (193°C). 3. Drain and dry the potato sticks really well, using a clean kitchen towel. Toss the fries with the oil in a bowl and then air fry the fries in the two air fryer baskets at 380°F (193°C) for 15 minutes, shaking the baskets a couple of times while they cook. 4. As soon as the fries are done, season them with salt and transfer to a plate. Serve them warm with ketchup or your favorite dip.

Shrimp Pirogues

Prep time: 15 minutes | Cook time: 4 to 5 minutes | Serves 8

12 ounces (340 g) small, peeled, and deveined raw shrimp
3 ounces (85 g) cream cheese, room temperature
2 tablespoons plain yogurt
1 teaspoon lemon juice
1 teaspoon dried dill weed, crushed
Salt, to taste
4 small hothouse cucumbers, each approximately 6 inches long

1. Pour 4 tablespoons water in bottom of two air fryer baskets. 2. Place shrimp in the two air fryer basket in single layer and air fry at 390ºF (199ºC) for 4 to 5 minutes, just until done. Watch carefully because shrimp cooks quickly, and overcooking makes it tough. 3. Chop shrimp into small pieces, no larger than ½ inch. Refrigerate while mixing the remaining ingredients. 4. With a fork, mash and whip the cream cheese until smooth. 5. Stir in the yogurt and beat until smooth. Stir in lemon juice, dill weed, and chopped shrimp. 6. Taste for seasoning. If needed, add ¼ to ½ teaspoon salt to suit your taste. 7. Store in refrigerator until serving time. 8. When ready to serve, wash and dry cucumbers and split them lengthwise. Scoop out the seeds and turn cucumbers upside down on paper towels to drain for 10 minutes. 9. Just before filling, wipe centers of cucumbers dry. Spoon the shrimp mixture into the pirogues and cut in half crosswise. Serve immediately.

Asian Five-Spice Wings

Prep time: 30 minutes | Cook time: 13 to 15 minutes | Serves 4

2 pounds (907 g) chicken wings
½ cup Asian-style salad dressing
2 tablespoons Chinese five-spice powder

1. Cut off wing tips and discard or freeze for stock. Cut remaining wing pieces in two at the joint. 2. Place wing pieces in a large sealable plastic bag. Pour in the Asian dressing, seal bag, and massage the marinade into the wings until well coated. Refrigerate for at least an hour. 3. Remove wings from bag, drain off excess marinade, and place wings in two air fryer baskets. 4. Air fry at 360ºF (182ºC) for 13 to 15 minutes or until juices run clear. About halfway through cooking time, shake the baskets or stir wings for more even cooking. 5. Transfer cooked wings to plate in a single layer. Sprinkle half of the Chinese five-spice powder on the wings, turn, and sprinkle other side with remaining seasoning.

Corn Dog Muffins

Prep time: 10 minutes | Cook time: 8 to 10 minutes | Makes 8 muffins

1¼ cups sliced kosher hotdogs (3 or 4, depending on size)
½ cup flour
½ cup yellow cornmeal
2 teaspoons baking powder
½ cup skim milk
1 egg
2 tablespoons canola oil
8 foil muffin cups, paper liners removed
Cooking spray
Mustard or your favorite dipping sauce

1. Slice each hotdog in half lengthwise, then cut in ¼-inch half-moon slices. Set aside. 2. Preheat the air fryer to 390ºF (199ºC). 3. In a large bowl, stir together flour, cornmeal, and baking powder. 4. In a small bowl, beat together the milk, egg, and oil until just blended. 5. Pour egg mixture into dry ingredients and stir with a spoon to mix well. 6. Stir in sliced hot dogs. 7. Spray the foil cups lightly with cooking spray. 8. Divide mixture evenly into muffin cups. 9. Place 8 muffin cups in the two air fryer baskets and cook for 5 minutes. 10. Reduce temperature to 360ºF (182ºC) and cook 3 to 5 minutes or until toothpick inserted in center of muffin comes out clean. 11. Serve with mustard or other sauces for dipping.

Pita Flatbread and Sweet Potato Chips

Prep time: 10 minutes | Cook time: 15 minutes | Serves 6

Pita Flatbread:
2 whole wheat pitas
2 tablespoons olive oil, divided
2 garlic cloves, minced
¼ teaspoon salt
½ cup canned artichoke hearts, sliced
¼ cup Kalamata olives
¼ cup shredded Parmesan
¼ cup crumbled feta
Chopped fresh parsley, for garnish (optional)
Sweet Potato Chips:
1 large sweet potato, sliced thin
⅛ teaspoon salt
2 tablespoons olive oil

Make the Pita Flatbread: (zone 1 basket)1. Preheat the air fryer to 380ºF(193ºC). 2. Brush each pita with 1 tablespoon olive oil, then sprinkle the minced garlic and salt over the top. 3. Distribute the artichoke hearts, olives, and cheeses evenly between the two pitas, and place both into the zone 1 air fryer to bake for 10 minutes. 4. Remove the pitas and cut them into 4 pieces each before serving. Sprinkle parsley over the top, if desired.
Make the Sweet Potato Chips (zone 2 basket): 1. Preheat the air fryer to 380ºF(193ºC). 2. In a small bowl, toss the sweet potatoes, salt, and olive oil together until the potatoes are well coated. 3. Put the sweet potato slices into the zone 2 air fryer basket and spread them out in a single layer. 4. Fry for 10 minutes. Stir, then air fry for 3 to 5 minutes more, or until the chips reach the preferred level of crispiness.

Bacon-Wrapped Shrimp and Jalapeño

Prep time: 20 minutes | Cook time: 26 minutes | Serves 8

24 large shrimp, peeled and deveined, about ¾ pound (340 g)
5 tablespoons barbecue sauce, divided
12 strips bacon, cut in half
24 small pickled jalapeño slices

1. Toss together the shrimp and 3 tablespoons of the barbecue sauce. Let stand for 15 minutes. Soak 24 wooden toothpicks in water for 10 minutes. Wrap 1 piece bacon around the shrimp and jalapeño slice, then secure with a toothpick. 2. Preheat the air fryer to 350ºF (177ºC). 3. Place the shrimp in the two air fryer baskets, spacing them ½ inch apart. Air fry for 10 minutes. Turn shrimp over with tongs and air fry for 3 minutes more, or until bacon is golden brown and shrimp are cooked through. 4. Brush with the remaining barbecue sauce and serve.

Chapter 8 Desserts

Chapter 8 Desserts

Vanilla Cookies with Hazelnuts

Prep time: 20 minutes | Cook time: 10 minutes | Serves 6

1 cup almond flour
½ cup coconut flour
1 teaspoon baking soda
1 teaspoon fine sea salt
1 stick butter
1 cup Swerve
2 teaspoons vanilla
2 eggs, at room temperature
1 cup hazelnuts, coarsely chopped

1. Preheat the air fryer to 350°F (177°C). 2. Mix the flour with the baking soda, and sea salt. 3. In the bowl of an electric mixer, beat the butter, Swerve, and vanilla until creamy. Fold in the eggs, one at a time, and mix until well combined. 4. Slowly and gradually, stir in the flour mixture. Finally, fold in the coarsely chopped hazelnuts. 5. Divide the dough into small balls using a large cookie scoop; drop onto the prepared cookie sheets. Bake in the two air fryer baskets for 10 minutes or until golden brown, rotating the pan once or twice through the cooking time. 6. Cool for a couple of minutes before removing to wire racks. Enjoy!

Butter Flax Cookies and Pumpkin Spice Pecans

Prep time: 30 minutes | Cook time: 20 minutes | Serves 8

Butter Flax Cookies:
8 ounces (227 g) almond meal
2 tablespoons flaxseed meal
1 ounce (28 g) monk fruit
1 teaspoon baking powder
A pinch of grated nutmeg
A pinch of coarse salt
1 large egg, room temperature.
1 stick butter, room temperature
1 teaspoon vanilla extract
Pumpkin Spice Pecans:
1 cup whole pecans
¼ cup granular erythritol
1 large egg white
½ teaspoon ground cinnamon
½ teaspoon pumpkin pie spice
½ teaspoon vanilla extract

Make the Butter Flax Cookies (zone 1 basket): 1. Mix the almond meal, flaxseed meal, monk fruit, baking powder, grated nutmeg, and salt in a bowl. 2. In a separate bowl, whisk the egg, butter, and vanilla extract. 3. Stir the egg mixture into dry mixture; mix to combine well or until it forms a nice, soft dough. 4. Roll your dough out and cut out with a cookie cutter of your choice. Bake in the preheated zone 1 air fryer basket at 350°F (177°C) for 10 minutes. Decrease the temperature to 330°F (166°C) and cook for 10 minutes longer. Bon appétit!
Make the Pumpkin Spice Pecans (zone 2 basket): 1. Toss all ingredients in a large bowl until pecans are coated. Place into the zone 2 air fryer basket. 2. Adjust the temperature to 300°F (149°C) and air fry for 6 minutes. 3. Toss two to three times during cooking. 4. Allow to cool completely. Store in an airtight container up to 3 days.

Coconut-Custard Pie

Prep time: 10 minutes | Cook time: 20 to 23 minutes | Serves 4

1 cup milk
¼ cup plus 2 tablespoons sugar
¼ cup biscuit baking mix
1 teaspoon vanilla
2 eggs
2 tablespoons melted butter
Cooking spray
½ cup shredded, sweetened coconut

1. Place all ingredients except coconut in a medium bowl. 2. Using a hand mixer, beat on high speed for 3 minutes. 3. Let sit for 5 minutes. 4. Preheat the zone 1 air fryer to 330°F (166°C). 5. Spray a baking pan with cooking spray and place pan in the zone 1 air fryer basket. 6. Pour filling into pan and sprinkle coconut over top. 7. Cook pie at 330°F (166°C) for 20 to 23 minutes or until center sets.

Coconut Macaroons

Prep time: 5 minutes | Cook time: 8 to 10 minutes | Makes 12 macaroons

1⅓ cups shredded, sweetened coconut
4½ teaspoons flour
2 tablespoons sugar
1 egg white
½ teaspoon almond extract

1. Preheat the air fryer to 330°F (166°C). 2. Mix all ingredients together. 3. Shape coconut mixture into 12 balls. 4. Place all 12 macaroons in the two air fryer baskets. They won't expand, so you can place them close together, but they shouldn't touch. 5. Air fry at 330°F (166°C) for 8 to 10 minutes, until golden.

Pecan and Cherry Stuffed Apples

Prep time: 10 minutes | Cook time: 20 minutes | Serves 4

4 apples (about 1¼ pounds / 567 g)
¼ cup chopped pecans
⅓ cup dried tart cherries
1 tablespoon melted butter
3 tablespoons brown sugar
¼ teaspoon allspice
Pinch salt
Ice cream, for serving

1. Cut off top ½ inch from each apple; reserve tops. With a melon baller, core through stem ends without breaking through the bottom. (Do not trim bases.) 2. Preheat the zone 1 air fryer basket to 350°F (177°C). Combine pecans, cherries, butter, brown sugar, allspice, and a pinch of salt. Stuff mixture into the hollow centers of the apples. Cover with apple tops. Put in the zone 1 air fryer basket, using tongs. Air fry for 20 to 25 minutes, or just until tender. 3. Serve warm with ice cream.

Baked Brazilian Pineapple

Prep time: 10 minutes | Cook time: 10 minutes | Serves 4

½ cup brown sugar
2 teaspoons ground cinnamon
1 small pineapple, peeled, cored, and cut into spears
3 tablespoons unsalted butter, melted

1. In a small bowl, mix the brown sugar and cinnamon until thoroughly combined. 2. Brush the pineapple spears with the melted butter. Sprinkle the cinnamon-sugar over the spears, pressing lightly to ensure it adheres well. 3. Place the spears in the two air fryer baskets in a single layer. Set the air fryer to 400°F (204°C) for 10 minutes. Halfway through the cooking time, brush the spears with butter. 4. The pineapple spears are done when they are heated through and the sugar is bubbling. Serve hot.

Apple Wedges with Apricots

Prep time: 5 minutes | Cook time: 15 to 18 minutes | Serves 4

4 large apples, peeled and sliced into 8 wedges
2 tablespoons olive oil
½ cup dried apricots, chopped
1 to 2 tablespoons sugar
½ teaspoon ground cinnamon

1. Preheat the air fryer to 350°F (180°C). 2. Toss the apple wedges with the olive oil in a mixing bowl until well coated. 3. Place the apple wedges in the two air fryer baskets and air fry for 12 to 15 minutes. 4. Sprinkle with the dried apricots and air fry for another 3 minutes. 5. Meanwhile, thoroughly combine the sugar and cinnamon in a small bowl. 6. Remove the apple wedges from the basket to a plate. Serve sprinkled with the sugar mixture.

Gluten-Free Spice Cookies

Prep time: 10 minutes | Cook time: 12 minutes | Serves 4

4 tablespoons (½ stick) unsalted butter, at room temperature
2 tablespoons agave nectar
1 large egg
2 tablespoons water
2½ cups almond flour
½ cup sugar
2 teaspoons ground ginger
1 teaspoon ground cinnamon
½ teaspoon freshly grated nutmeg
1 teaspoon baking soda
¼ teaspoon kosher salt

1. Line the bottom of the zone 1 air fryer basket with parchment paper cut to fit. 2. In a large bowl using a hand mixer, beat together the butter, agave, egg, and water on medium speed until light and fluffy. 3. Add the almond flour, sugar, ginger, cinnamon, nutmeg, baking soda, and salt. Beat on low speed until well combined. 4. Roll the dough into 2-tablespoon balls and arrange them on the parchment paper in the zone 1 basket. (They don't really spread too much, but try to leave a little room between them.) Set the temperature to 325°F (163°C) for 12 minutes, or until the tops of cookies are lightly browned. 5. Transfer to a wire rack and let cool completely. Store in an airtight container for up to a week.

Peach Fried Pies

Prep time: 15 minutes | Cook time: 20 minutes | Makes 8 pies

1 (14.75-ounce / 418-g) can sliced peaches in heavy syrup
1 teaspoon ground cinnamon
1 tablespoon cornstarch
1 large egg
All-purpose flour, for dusting
2 refrigerated piecrusts

1. Reserving 2 tablespoons of syrup, drain the peaches well. Chop the peaches into bite-size pieces, transfer to a medium bowl, and stir in the cinnamon. 2. In a small bowl, stir together the reserved peach juice and cornstarch until dissolved. Stir this slurry into the peaches. 3. In another small bowl, beat the egg. 4. Dust a cutting board or work surface with flour and spread the piecrusts on the prepared surface. Using a knife, cut each crust into 4 squares (8 squares total). 5. Place 2 tablespoons of peaches onto each dough square. Fold the dough in half and seal the edges. Using a pastry brush, spread the beaten egg on both sides of each hand pie. Using a knife, make 2 thin slits in the top of each pie. 6. Preheat the air fryer to 350°F (177°C). 7. Line the two air fryer baskets with parchment paper. Place 4 pies on a piece of parchment. 8. Cook for 10 minutes. Flip the pies, brush with beaten egg, and cook for 5 minutes more.

Crustless Peanut Butter Cheesecake and Homemade Mint Pie

Prep time: 30 minutes | Cook time: 15 minutes | Serves 4

Crustless Peanut Butter Cheesecake:
4 ounces (113 g) cream cheese, softened
2 tablespoons confectioners' erythritol
1 tablespoon all-natural, no-sugar-added peanut butter
½ teaspoon vanilla extract
1 large egg, whisked

Homemade Mint Pie:
1 tablespoon instant coffee
2 tablespoons almond butter, softened
2 tablespoons erythritol
1 teaspoon dried mint
3 eggs, beaten
1 teaspoon spearmint, dried
4 teaspoons coconut flour
Cooking spray

Make the Crustless Peanut Butter Cheesecake (zone 1 basket): 1. In a medium bowl, mix cream cheese and erythritol until smooth. Add peanut butter and vanilla, mixing until smooth. Add egg and stir just until combined. 2. Spoon mixture into an ungreased springform pan and place into the zone 1 air fryer basket. Adjust the temperature to 300°F (149°C) and bake for 10 minutes. Edges will be firm, but center will be mostly set with only a small amount of jiggle when done. 3. Let pan cool at room temperature 30 minutes, cover with plastic wrap, then place into refrigerator at least 2 hours. Serve chilled.

Make the Homemade Mint Pie (zone 2 basket): 1. Spray the zone 2 air fryer basket with cooking spray. 2. Then mix all ingredients in the mixer bowl. 3. When you get a smooth mixture, transfer it in the zone 2 air fryer basket. Flatten it gently. Cook the pie at 365°F (185°C) for 25 minutes.

Butter and Chocolate Chip Cookies

Prep time: 20 minutes | Cook time: 11 minutes | Serves 8

1 stick butter, at room temperature	⅓ cup cocoa powder, unsweetened
1¼ cups Swerve	1½ teaspoons baking powder
¼ cup chunky peanut butter	¼ teaspoon ground cinnamon
1 teaspoon vanilla paste	¼ teaspoon ginger
1 fine almond flour	½ cup chocolate chips, unsweetened
⅔ cup coconut flour	

1. In a mixing dish, beat the butter and Swerve until creamy and uniform. Stir in the peanut butter and vanilla. 2. In another mixing dish, thoroughly combine the flour, cocoa powder, baking powder, cinnamon, and ginger. 3. Add the flour mixture to the peanut butter mixture; mix to combine well. Afterwards, fold in the chocolate chips. Drop by large spoonfuls onto two parchment-lined air fryer baskets. Bake at 365°F (185°C) for 11 minutes or until golden brown on the top. Bon appétit!

Vanilla Scones

Prep time: 20 minutes | Cook time: 10 minutes | Serves 6

4 ounces (113 g) coconut flour	¼ cup heavy cream
½ teaspoon baking powder	1 teaspoon vanilla extract
1 teaspoon apple cider vinegar	1 tablespoon erythritol
2 teaspoons mascarpone	Cooking spray

1. In the mixing bowl, mix coconut flour with baking powder, apple cider vinegar, mascarpone, heavy cream, vanilla extract, and erythritol. 2. Knead the dough and cut into scones. 3. Then put them in the two air fryer baskets and sprinkle with cooking spray. 4. Cook the vanilla scones at 365°F (185°C) for 10 minutes.

Almond Butter Cookie Balls and Coconut Flour Cake

Prep time: 15 minutes | Cook time: 25 minutes | Serves 9

Almond Butter Cookie Balls:	½ teaspoon ground cinnamon
1 cup almond butter	Coconut Flour Cake:
1 large egg	2 tablespoons salted butter, melted
1 teaspoon vanilla extract	⅓ cup coconut flour
¼ cup low-carb protein powder	2 large eggs, whisked
¼ cup powdered erythritol	½ cup granular erythritol
¼ cup shredded unsweetened coconut	1 teaspoon baking powder
¼ cup low-carb, sugar-free chocolate chips	1 teaspoon vanilla extract
	½ cup sour cream

Almond Butter Cookie Balls (zone 1 basket): 1. In a large bowl, mix almond butter and egg. Add in vanilla, protein powder, and erythritol. 2. Fold in coconut, chocolate chips, and cinnamon. Roll into 1-inch balls. Place balls into a round baking pan and put into the zone 1 air fryer basket. 3. Adjust the temperature to 320°F (160°C) and bake for 10 minutes. 4. Allow to cool completely. Store in an airtight container in the refrigerator up to 4 days.
Coconut Flour Cake (zone 2 basket): 1. Mix all ingredients in a large bowl. Pour batter into an ungreased round nonstick baking dish. 2. Place baking dish into the zone 2 air fryer basket. Adjust the temperature to 300°F (149°C) and bake for 25 minutes. The cake will be dark golden on top, and a toothpick inserted in the center should come out clean when done. 3. Let cool in dish 15 minutes before slicing and serving.

Simple Pineapple Sticks and Honeyed Roasted Apples with Walnuts

Prep time: 10 minutes | Cook time: 15 minutes | Serves 7

Simple Pineapple Sticks:	¼ cup certified gluten-free rolled oats
½ fresh pineapple, cut into sticks	2 tablespoons honey
¼ cup desiccated coconut	½ teaspoon ground cinnamon
Honeyed Roasted Apples with Walnuts:	2 tablespoons chopped walnuts
	Pinch salt
2 Granny Smith apples	1 tablespoon olive oil

Make the Simple Pineapple Sticks (zone 1 basket): 1. Preheat the zone 1 air fryer basket to 400°F (204°C). 2. Coat the pineapple sticks in the desiccated coconut and put each one in the zone 1 air fryer basket. 3. Air fry for 10 minutes. 4. Serve immediately
Make the Honeyed Roasted Apples with Walnuts (zone 2 basket): 1. Preheat the zone 2 air fryer basket to 380°F (193°C). 2. Core the apples and slice them in half. 3. In a medium bowl, mix together the oats, honey, cinnamon, walnuts, salt, and olive oil. 4. Scoop a quarter of the oat mixture onto the top of each half apple. 5. Place the apples in the zone 2 air fryer basket, and roast for 12 to 15 minutes, or until the apples are fork-tender.

Cream-Filled Sandwich Cookies

Prep time: 8 minutes | Cook time: 8 minutes | Makes 8 cookies

Oil, for spraying	8 cream-filled sandwich cookies
1 (8-ounce / 227-g) can refrigerated crescent rolls	1 tablespoon confectioners' sugar
¼ cup milk	

1. Line the two air fryer baskets with parchment and spray lightly with oil. 2. Unroll the crescent dough and separate it into 8 triangles. Lay out the triangles on a work surface. 3. Pour the milk into a shallow bowl. Quickly dip each cookie in the milk, then place in the center of a dough triangle. 4. Wrap the dough around the cookie, cutting off any excess and pinching the ends to seal. You may be able to combine the excess into enough dough to cover additional cookies, if desired. 5. Place the wrapped cookies in the prepared baskets, seam-side down, and spray lightly with oil. 6. Bake at 350°F (177°C) for 4 minutes, flip, spray with oil, and cook for another 3 to 4 minutes, or until puffed and golden brown. 7. Dust with the confectioners' sugar and serve.

Fried Cheesecake Bites

Prep time: 30 minutes | Cook time: 2 minutes | Makes 16 bites

8 ounces (227 g) cream cheese, softened
½ cup plus 2 tablespoons Swerve, divided
4 tablespoons heavy cream, divided
½ teaspoon vanilla extract
½ cup almond flour

1. In a stand mixer fitted with a paddle attachment, beat the cream cheese, ½ cup of the Swerve, 2 tablespoons of the heavy cream, and the vanilla until smooth. Using a small ice-cream scoop, divide the mixture into 16 balls and arrange them on a rimmed baking sheet lined with parchment paper. Freeze for 45 minutes until firm. 2. Line the two air fryer baskets with parchment paper and preheat the air fryer to 350°F (177°C). 3. In a small shallow bowl, combine the almond flour with the remaining 2 tablespoons Swerve. 4. In another small shallow bowl, place the remaining 2 tablespoons cream. 5. One at a time, dip the frozen cheesecake balls into the cream and then roll in the almond flour mixture, pressing lightly to form an even coating. Arrange the balls in a single layer in the two air fryer baskets, leaving room between them. Air fry for 2 minutes until the coating is lightly browned.

Applesauce and Chocolate Brownies

Prep time: 10 minutes | Cook time: 15 minutes | Serves 8

¼ cup unsweetened cocoa powder
¼ cup all-purpose flour
¼ teaspoon kosher salt
½ teaspoons baking powder
3 tablespoons unsalted butter, melted
½ cup granulated sugar
1 large egg
3 tablespoons unsweetened applesauce
¼ cup miniature semisweet chocolate chips
Coarse sea salt, to taste

1. Preheat the zone 1 air fryer to 300°F (149°C). 2. In a large bowl, whisk together the cocoa powder, all-purpose flour, kosher salt, and baking powder. 3. In a separate large bowl, combine the butter, granulated sugar, egg, and applesauce, then use a spatula to fold in the cocoa powder mixture and the chocolate chips until well combined. 4. Spray a baking pan with nonstick cooking spray, then pour the mixture into the pan. Place the pan in the zone 1 air fryer basket and bake for 15 minutes or until a toothpick comes out clean when inserted in the middle. 5. Remove the brownies from the air fryer, sprinkle some coarse sea salt on top, and allow to cool in the pan on a wire rack for 20 minutes before cutting and serving.

Caramelized Fruit Skewers

Prep time: 10 minutes | Cook time: 3 to 5 minutes | Serves 4

2 peaches, peeled, pitted, and thickly sliced
3 plums, halved and pitted
3 nectarines, halved and pitted
1 tablespoon honey
½ teaspoon ground cinnamon
¼ teaspoon ground allspice
Pinch cayenne pepper
Special Equipment:
8 metal skewers

1. Preheat the air fryer to 400°F (204°C). 2. Thread, alternating peaches, plums, and nectarines, onto the metal skewers that fit into the air fryer. 3. Thoroughly combine the honey, cinnamon, allspice, and cayenne in a small bowl. Brush generously the glaze over the fruit skewers. 4. Transfer the fruit skewers to the two air fryer baskets. 5. Air fry for 3 to 5 minutes, or until the fruit is caramelized. 6. Remove from the baskets and repeat with the remaining fruit skewers. 7. Let the fruit skewers rest for 5 minutes before serving.

Baked Peaches with Yogurt and Blueberries

Prep time: 10 minutes | Cook time: 7 to 11 minutes | Serves 6

3 peaches, peeled, halved, and pitted
2 tablespoons packed brown sugar
1 cup plain Greek yogurt
¼ teaspoon ground cinnamon
1 teaspoon pure vanilla extract
1 cup fresh blueberries

1. Preheat the zone 1 air fryer basket to 380°F (193°C). 2. Arrange the peaches in the zone 1 air fryer basket, cut-side up. Top with a generous sprinkle of brown sugar. 3. Bake in the zone 1 air fryer basket for 7 to 11 minutes, or until the peaches are lightly browned and caramelized. 4. Meanwhile, whisk together the yogurt, cinnamon, and vanilla in a small bowl until smooth. 5. Remove the peaches from the basket to a plate. Serve topped with the yogurt mixture and fresh blueberries.

Chapter 9 Staples, Sauces, Dips, and Dressings

Chapter 9 Staples, Sauces, Dips, and Dressings

Homemade Remoulade Sauce

Prep time: 5 minutes | Cook time: 0 minutes | Serves 4

¾ cup mayonnaise
1 garlic clove, minced
2 tablespoons mustard
1 teaspoon horseradish
1 teaspoon Cajun seasoning
1 teaspoon dill pickle juice
½ teaspoon paprika
¼ teaspoon hot pepper sauce

1. Whisk together all the ingredients in a small bowl until completely mixed. 2. It can be used as a delicious dip for veggies, a sandwich or burger spread, or you can serve it with chicken fingers for a dipping sauce.

Green Basil Dressing
Prep time: 10 minutes | Cook time: 0 minutes | Makes 1 cup
1 avocado, peeled and pitted
¼ cup sour cream
¼ cup extra-virgin olive oil
¼ cup chopped fresh basil
1 tablespoon freshly squeezed lime juice
1 teaspoon minced garlic
Sea salt and freshly ground black pepper, to taste

1. Place the avocado, sour cream, olive oil, basil, lime juice, and garlic in a food processor and pulse until smooth, scraping down the sides of the bowl once during processing. 2. Season the dressing with salt and pepper. 3. Keep the dressing in an airtight container in the refrigerator for 1 to 2 weeks.

Cauliflower Alfredo Sauce

Prep time: 2 minutes | Cook time: 0 minutes | Makes 4 cups

2 tablespoons olive oil
6 garlic cloves, minced
3 cups unsweetened almond milk
1 (1-pound / 454-g) head cauliflower, cut into florets
1 teaspoon salt
¼ teaspoon freshly ground black pepper
Juice of 1 lemon
4 tablespoons nutritional yeast

1. In a medium saucepan, heat the olive oil over medium-high heat. Add the garlic and sauté for 1 minute or until fragrant. Add the almond milk, stir, and bring to a boil. 2. Gently add the cauliflower. Stir in the salt and pepper and return to a boil. Continue cooking over medium-high heat for 5 minutes or until the cauliflower is soft. Stir frequently and reduce heat if needed to prevent the liquid from boiling over. 3. Carefully transfer the cauliflower and cooking liquid to a food processor, using a slotted spoon to scoop out the larger pieces of cauliflower before pouring in the liquid. Add the lemon and nutritional yeast and blend for 1 to 2 minutes until smooth. 4. Serve immediately.

Blue Cheese Dressing

Prep time: 5 minutes | Cook time: 0 minutes | Serves 12

¾ cup sugar-free mayonnaise
¼ cup sour cream
½ cup heavy (whipping) cream
1 teaspoon minced garlic
1 tablespoon freshly squeezed lemon juice
1 tablespoon apple cider vinegar
1 teaspoon hot sauce
½ teaspoon sea salt
4 ounces (113 g) blue cheese, crumbled (about ¾ cup)

1. In a medium bowl, whisk together the mayonnaise, sour cream, and heavy cream. 2. Stir in the garlic, lemon juice, apple cider vinegar, hot sauce, and sea salt. 3. Add the blue cheese crumbles, and stir until well combined. 4. Transfer to an airtight container, and refrigerate for up to 1 week.

Hemp Dressing

Prep time: 5 minutes | Cook time: 0 minutes | Makes 12 tablespoons

½ cup white wine vinegar
¼ cup tahini
¼ cup water
1 tablespoon hemp seeds
½ tablespoon freshly squeezed lemon juice
1 teaspoon garlic powder
1 teaspoon dried oregano
1 teaspoon dried basil
1 teaspoon red pepper flakes
½ teaspoon onion powder
½ teaspoon pink Himalayan salt
½ teaspoon freshly ground black pepper

1. In a bowl, combine all the ingredients and whisk until mixed well.

Orange Dijon Dressing

Prep time: 5 minutes | Cook time: 0 minutes | Serves 2

¼ cup extra-virgin olive oil
2 tablespoons freshly squeezed orange juice
1 orange, zested
1 teaspoon garlic powder
¾ teaspoon za'atar seasoning
½ teaspoon salt
¼ teaspoon Dijon mustard
Freshly ground black pepper, to taste

1. In a jar, combine the olive oil, orange juice and zest, garlic powder, za'atar, salt, and mustard. Season with pepper and shake vigorously until completely mixed.

Pecan Tartar Sauce

Prep time: 10 minutes | Cook time: 10 minutes | Makes 1¼ cups

4 tablespoons pecans, finely chopped
½ cup sour cream
½ cup mayonnaise
½ teaspoon grated lemon zest

1½ tablespoons freshly squeezed lemon juice
2½ tablespoons chopped fresh parsley
1 teaspoon paprika
2 tablespoons chopped dill pickle

1. Preheat the air fryer to 325°F (163°C). Spread the pecans in a single layer on a parchment sheet lightly spritzed with oil. Place the pecans in the air fryer. Air fry for 7 to 10 minutes, stirring every 2 minutes. Let cool. 2. In a medium bowl, mix the sour cream, mayonnaise, lemon zest, and lemon juice until blended. 3. Stir in the parsley paprika, dill pickle, and pecans. Cover and refrigerate to chill for at least 1 hour to blend the flavors. This sauce should be used within 2 weeks.

Avocado Dressing

Prep time: 5 minutes | Cook time: 0 minutes | Makes 12 tablespoons

1 large avocado, pitted and peeled
½ cup water
2 tablespoons tahini
2 tablespoons freshly squeezed lemon juice
1 teaspoon dried basil

1 teaspoon white wine vinegar
1 garlic clove
¼ teaspoon pink Himalayan salt
¼ teaspoon freshly ground black pepper

1. Combine all the ingredients in a food processor and blend until smooth.

Sweet Ginger Teriyaki Sauce

Prep time: 5 minutes | Cook time: 0 minutes | Serves 4

¼ cup pineapple juice
¼ cup low-sodium soy sauce
2 tablespoons packed brown sugar

1 tablespoon arrowroot powder or cornstarch
1 tablespoon grated fresh ginger
1 teaspoon garlic powder

1. Mix together all the ingredients in a small bowl and whisk to incorporate. 2. Serve immediately, or transfer to an airtight container and refrigerate until ready to use.

Appendix 1 Measurement Conversion Chart

MEASUREMENT CONVERSION CHART

VOLUME EQUIVALENTS (DRY)

US STANDARD	METRIC (APPROXIMATE)
1/8 teaspoon	0.5 mL
1/4 teaspoon	1 mL
1/2 teaspoon	2 mL
3/4 teaspoon	4 mL
1 teaspoon	5 mL
1 tablespoon	15 mL
1/4 cup	59 mL
1/2 cup	118 mL
3/4 cup	177 mL
1 cup	235 mL
2 cups	475 mL
3 cups	700 mL
4 cups	1 L

VOLUME EQUIVALENTS (LIQUID)

US STANDARD	US STANDARD (OUNCES)	METRIC (APPROXIMATE)
2 tablespoons	1 fl.oz.	30 mL
1/4 cup	2 fl.oz.	60 mL
1/2 cup	4 fl.oz.	120 mL
1 cup	8 fl.oz.	240 mL
1 1/2 cup	12 fl.oz.	355 mL
2 cups or 1 pint	16 fl.oz.	475 mL
4 cups or 1 quart	32 fl.oz.	1 L
1 gallon	128 fl.oz.	4 L

TEMPERATURES EQUIVALENTS

FAHRENHEIT (F)	CELSIUS (C) (APPROXIMATE)
225 °F	107 °C
250 °F	120 °C
275 °F	135 °C
300 °F	150 °C
325 °F	160 °C
350 °F	180 °C
375 °F	190 °C
400 °F	205 °C
425 °F	220 °C
450 °F	235 °C
475 °F	245 °C
500 °F	260 °C

WEIGHT EQUIVALENTS

US STANDARD	METRIC (APPROXIMATE)
1 ounce	28 g
2 ounces	57 g
5 ounces	142 g
10 ounces	284 g
15 ounces	425 g
16 ounces (1 pound)	455 g
1.5 pounds	680 g
2 pounds	907 g

Appendix 2 Air Fryer Cooking Chart

Air Fryer Cooking Chart

Beef

Item	Temp (°F)	Time (mins)	Item	Temp (°F)	Time (mins)
Beef Eye Round Roast (4 lbs.)	400 °F	45 to 55	Meatballs (1-inch)	370 °F	7
Burger Patty (4 oz.)	370 °F	16 to 20	Meatballs (3-inch)	380 °F	10
Filet Mignon (8 oz.)	400 °F	18	Ribeye, bone-in (1-inch, 8 oz)	400 °F	10 to 15
Flank Steak (1.5 lbs.)	400 °F	12	Sirloin steaks (1-inch, 12 oz)	400 °F	9 to 14
Flank Steak (2 lbs.)	400 °F	20 to 28			

Chicken

Item	Temp (°F)	Time (mins)	Item	Temp (°F)	Time (mins)
Breasts, bone in (1 ¼ lb.)	370 °F	25	Legs, bone-in (1 ¾ lb.)	380 °F	30
Breasts, boneless (4 oz)	380 °F	12	Thighs, boneless (1 ½ lb.)	380 °F	18 to 20
Drumsticks (2 ½ lb.)	370 °F	20	Wings (2 lb.)	400 °F	12
Game Hen (halved 2 lb.)	390 °F	20	Whole Chicken	360 °F	75
Thighs, bone-in (2 lb.)	380 °F	22	Tenders	360 °F	8 to 10

Pork & Lamb

Item	Temp (°F)	Time (mins)	Item	Temp (°F)	Time (mins)
Bacon (regular)	400 °F	5 to 7	Pork Tenderloin	370 °F	15
Bacon (thick cut)	400 °F	6 to 10	Sausages	380 °F	15
Pork Loin (2 lb.)	360 °F	55	Lamb Loin Chops (1-inch thick)	400 °F	8 to 12
Pork Chops, bone in (1-inch, 6.5 oz)	400 °F	12	Rack of Lamb (1.5 – 2 lb.)	380 °F	22

Fish & Seafood

Item	Temp (°F)	Time (mins)	Item	Temp (°F)	Time (mins)
Calamari (8 oz)	400 °F	4	Tuna Steak	400 °F	7 to 10
Fish Fillet (1-inch, 8 oz)	400 °F	10	Scallops	400 °F	5 to 7
Salmon, fillet (6 oz)	380 °F	12	Shrimp	400 °F	5
Swordfish steak	400 °F	10			

Air Fryer Cooking Chart

Vegetables					
INGREDIENT	AMOUNT	PREPARATION	OIL	TEMP	COOK TIME
Asparagus	2 bunches	Cut in half, trim stems	2 Tbsp	420°F	12-15 mins
Beets	1½ lbs	Peel, cut in ½-inch cubes	1 Tbsp	390°F	28-30 mins
Bell peppers (for roasting)	4 peppers	Cut in quarters, remove seeds	1 Tbsp	400°F	15-20 mins
Broccoli	1 large head	Cut in 1-2-inch florets	1 Tbsp	400°F	15-20 mins
Brussels sprouts	1 lb	Cut in half, remove stems	1 Tbsp	425°F	15-20 mins
Carrots	1 lb	Peel, cut in ¼-inch rounds	1 Tbsp	425°F	10-15 mins
Cauliflower	1 head	Cut in 1-2-inch florets	2 Tbsp	400°F	20-22 mins
Corn on the cob	7 ears	Whole ears, remove husks	1 Tbps	400°F	14-17 mins
Green beans	1 bag (12 oz)	Trim	1 Tbps	420°F	18-20 mins
Kale (for chips)	4 oz	Tear into pieces, remove stems	None	325°F	5-8 mins
Mushrooms	16 oz	Rinse, slice thinly	1 Tbps	390°F	25-30 mins
Potatoes, russet	1½ lbs	Cut in 1-inch wedges	1 Tbps	390°F	25-30 mins
Potatoes, russet	1 lb	Hand-cut fries, soak 30 mins in cold water, then pat dry	½ -3 Tbps	400°F	25-28 mins
Potatoes, sweet	1 lb	Hand-cut fries, soak 30 mins in cold water, then pat dry	1 Tbps	400°F	25-28 mins
Zucchini	1 lb	Cut in eighths lengthwise, then cut in half	1 Tbps	400°F	15-20 mins

Printed in Great Britain
by Amazon